W9-BDB-826

PLAY THE GAME

Squash

Squash

JAMES MEDLYCOTT

Hamlyn

London · New York · Sydney · Toronto

Acknowledgments

Photography by Don Morley/All-Sport
The photographs were taken at the Leatherhead Leisure Centre, holders of the
Sports Council's Regional Award for Good Management 1976–77. The two
players photographed are A. J. (Seumus) Buchanan and Stephen Key. Seumus
Buchanan, a Squash Rackets Association advanced coach and marker/referee, is
Surrey Coach with responsibility for the Surrey Junior Squash training squad;
16-year old Stephen Key, who posed for all the how-not-to-do-it shots, is
actually a member of the Surrey Junior Under-19 Squash Squad. The author
and publisher gratefully acknowledge the generous assistance of all concerned.

The graphs on page 51 were first published in D. S. Muckle's paper entitled
'Glucose Syrup Ingestion and Team Performance in Soccer' (British Journal of
Sports Medicine, volume 7, no. 3/4, 1973). The copyright is held jointly by
Mr Muckle, M.B.B.S., F.R.C.S., M.S., and the B.J.S.M.

The 'Popmobility' training sequences on pages 55–6 are reproduced by kind
permission of Robinsons Barley Waters, Ken Woolcott, and Bond Clarkson
Russell Limited.

The diagrams were drawn by David Watson.

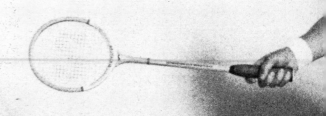

Published by
The Hamlyn Publishing Group Limited
London · New York · Sydney · Toronto
Astronaut House, Feltham, Middlesex, England

Originally published as *How to play Squash*

ISBN 0 600 34763 X

Printed in Italy

Foreword

Squash rackets is an enjoyable, fast, dynamic game of constant movement and effort. Though a sound grasp of tactics is important, squash is essentially a physical activity in which techniques are learned and developed by conditioning the reflexes rather than through conscious thought. In consequence the amount that can be understood by reading and then transferred to effective action is limited. Too much detail is likely to confuse, too little necessitates interpretations which are probably beyond the understanding of novices and intermediates.

This book has been written with those limitations strictly in mind. Its contents have been considered and refined so that they can safely make the journey from understanding to performance. Only one demand is made – the reader must digest each chapter slowly and carefully before trying out the recommendations and advice with even greater care and deeper concentration than he or she might give to a competitive game. In that way techniques and tactics can be absorbed and satisfaction achieved through steady improvement.

The book has been written from a right-handed player's viewpoint. Left-handers will have to reverse all directions when reading specific instructions.

J.M.

Contents

Chapter One
Introducing the Game

Why Squash?

Remember Mae West's immortal words: 'It isn't the men in your life that count. It's the life in your men.'? Rework that sentiment just a little – 'It isn't the years in your life that count. It's the life in your years' – and you know why I recommend squash rackets.

With more and more people in the West surviving to attain the biblical three score years and ten, it becomes increasingly important that those additional years should prove rich in enjoyment. Good health plays an important part in your ability to enjoy life and the road to good health lies through sensible exercise. Squash rackets, henceforth squash, is an ideal method of obtaining that health-building exercise. An indoor game, it is totally unaffected by hail, sleet, rain, or snow. You and I can arrange a game for the third Sunday in March 1990 with the certain knowledge that inclement weather will not stop us playing.

Currently the game is enjoying an unprecedented boom, and deservedly so. This is an era when time seems at a premium and the internal combustion engine is threatening to atrophy the primary leg muscles of tens of millions of Westerners. Squash packs a good deal of pleasurable exercise into 40 minutes or so with minimal danger to health, providing you play opponents of a similar standard to yourself. It challenges your skill, tests your nerve, and stretches your imagination. Could there be a better antidote to the monotony which our industrial society often imposes upon us?

The Court

One of the newest of the racket games, squash is normally played in a rectangular, enclosed court 9·75 metres (32 feet) long by 6·40 metres (21 feet) wide. See Diagram 1 on page 8. Singles, one against one, is customary but rules exist for doubles.

The net of tennis and badminton is replaced by the 'tin', a piece of resonant material, usually metal, which runs the width of the front wall. Along the top of the tin is a piece of wood called the 'board'. The distance from the floor to the top of this board is 0·48 metres (19 inches), and it projects not less than 13 millimetres (½ inch), nor more than 25 millimetres (1 inch), from the front wall. The different sound made by the ball whenever it hits this section is an additional proof for players and onlookers that a shot has been 'hit down'.

A red line is drawn from a point 4·57 metres (15 feet) above floor level at each end of the front wall to points 2·13 metres (7 feet) high at each end of the back wall; those points are joined by the continuation of the side-wall lines across the front and back walls. Any ball hitting a wall on or above the boundary or out-of-court

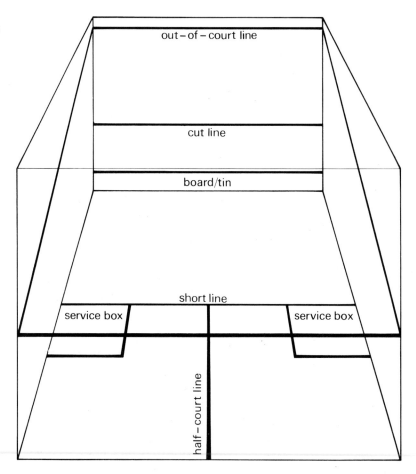

out – of – court line

cut line

board/tin

short line

service box

service box

half – court line

line is 'out'. Note that this differs from tennis, in which a line ball is 'in'. There is another red line drawn across the front wall; called the 'cut line', it is 1·83 metres (6 feet) above the floor and 2·74 metres (9 feet) below the front-wall boundary line.

The floor of the court is divided by one line (the 'short line') running parallel with the front and back walls 5·49 metres (18 feet) from the front wall. The back part of the court is divided into two equal sections by a line (the 'half-court line') running parallel with the side walls from the back wall to the short line. These two segments of the court each contain a 'service box', an area 1·60 metres (5 feet 3 inches) square, adjacent to the side wall, its front line being formed by part of the short line.

The Game

Each exchange of shots, or rally, begins with 'service', that is with a player releasing the ball from his or her hand and hitting it against the front wall above the cut line. To be 'good' the ball served must first hit that front wall above the cut line – no matter how many other walls it hits after doing so. Equally, should the ball served then touch the floor, it must fall within the back quarter of the court opposite the service box from which the service was delivered, whether or not it hits the side or back walls first.

As in tennis, the server is allowed one 'fault'. Unlike tennis, the receiver may hit the served ball before it bounces – that's called 'volleying' – and he or she may also elect to play the ball even if it is a fault. All lines other than the continuous boundary line are disregarded once the served ball has been accepted and struck by the receiver.

The rally continues with each player hitting the ball in turn until:

1 one of the players is unable to reach the ball and hit it onto the front wall above the tin before it has bounced twice;
2 the ball goes out of court, hitting one of the walls above the red boundary line;
3 the ball in play touches the opponent or anything worn or carried by the opponent and so is prevented from being a good return; or
4 the striker hits the ball twice.

Inevitably, doubts about shots sometimes arise, and when these cannot be resolved it is customary to 'play a let', i.e. replay the rally. There is one unusual way a point can be won or, more precisely, lost and that is when a player obstructs another from making a shot freely, whether or not the obstruction is intentional.

Only the player 'hand-in' – the server – can score points, and he or she continues serving alternately from the two service boxes until the receiver wins a rally. This is 'hand-out' for the player who was serving and 'hand-in' for the opponent, who can now start scoring.

The first player to score 9 points wins the game except when the score reaches 8-all. In this situation the receiver may 'set' the game to 10 points; otherwise, the next player to score a point wins the game. A match is usually the 'best of five games', i.e. the first player to win three games is the victor.

Equipment and Clothing

By now you should be ready to go on court by yourself and practise gently hitting the ball against the front wall, keeping it going as long as possible while you gather some sense of the 'feel'. If you already play tennis or badminton, you may experience difficulty in maintaining a rally, no matter how gently you hit your shots.

The reason is simple: a difference in distance between your hand and the middle of the racket head. In tennis approximately 540 millimetres (21¼ inches) separate the end of the racket handle from the centre of the racket face. In squash that distance is lengthened by roughly 38 millimetres (1½ inches) and complete adjustment presents problems to some people for a short while.

The ball used may add to your bewilderment: it can come in four different types, specified by dots of yellow, white, red, or blue. The dot indicates the speed of the ball, yellow being the slowest and blue the fastest. The continual crashing of the ball against the players' rackets and the walls warms it up, so increasing its inner temperature. It is commonplace in championship play for two evenly matched, hard-hitting opponents to shatter one or more balls during the course of a match. This hotting up and bursting cycle is normally confined to top-class play but, before bursting, the ball gradually becomes more lively, bouncing more easily so that the time between its first and second bounce continually lengthens. This gives active movers a better chance of reaching their opponents' best shots with the result that many contests at championship level are mainly battles of attrition in which the fitter and more mobile player frequently wears down a superior stroke-making opponent.

Beginners and novices are unlikely to hit sufficiently hard to warm up a yellow-dot ball so blue-dot balls should be their choice. As they progress they can change to red, then white, and finally yellow, when their shot-making equals their speed and stamina.

Choice of racket poses another problem. The aim of any player, beginner or advanced, should be to keep as many returns as possible slithering along the side walls. However, any beginner seeking to achieve this ideal must increase his or her chances of hitting the wall and breaking the racket. As technical skill develops, the ability to hit shots near the wall without touching it improves. This takes time, however, so beginners and probably intermediate players too should choose one of the many less expensive rackets obtainable in shops today. Be satisfied at first with one strung to a moderate tension as this will help to increase the amount of time the ball is actually in contact with the strings. Touch, or 'feel' if you prefer, is a product of time. The longer the ball and racket strings are in contact, the better the feel of the ball and, consequently, the control. When touch becomes more certain and the importance of power increases, it will probably be advisable to change to a racket with tighter strings.

Weights vary very little and the same is true of balance. Before buying, try out as many rackets belonging to friends as possible, always promising to pay for damage, of course. Note the characteristics of any you like especially and, when you finally go to a store, banish the self-consciousness that inhibits you from making some full-blooded though imaginary strokes before taking your final decision to buy and handing your cash over the counter.

Grip size is important. If it is too small, you will need to over-clench your hand. If it is too large, your wrist action may be slightly inhibited and squash strokes demand considerable flexibility of wrist if they are to be effective. However, do not worry too much about these warnings. On the whole, grip sizes do not vary so tremendously that you are likely to make a purchase which is too far from the theoretically perfect weight, balance, and grip size for you to become accustomed to it.

Man-made strings may not contribute as much to the 'feel' as those extracted from animals, usually lamb or sheep gut. On the other hand, they are far more durable and few beginners and

White kit and white socks and shoes, essentially non-black soles, are the usual rule for squash. Clothes with a high percentage of cotton or wool are the best because they absorb perspiration

novices are sufficiently adept to benefit significantly from insisting on the higher-priced, natural stringing.

The handle of a racket or, to be precise, the part one holds is normally covered with leather or a similar material, or with towelling. The latter feels softer to the hand at first but sweat eventually makes it harder. Choice finally comes down to personal preference.

Clothing is important. The essential point is to keep warm before play begins and during the preliminary, loosening knock-up, in which the muscles slowly gain elasticity and so can stretch without damage. Once your warm-up sweater or tracksuit top and, perhaps, trousers have been removed, you should normally reveal white kit (shorts, shirt, skirt, or dress) and white socks and shoes.

All garments should fit loosely, though not like a sack. Certainly you must have complete freedom to start, stop, bend, and twist every 2 seconds or so for the 40 minutes which is the usual length of a session booked at a club or public centre, but there is un-doubtedly a psychological advantage in looking smart on court.

11

If you are going all out, you are likely to sweat profusely and this perspiration must be absorbed; if it is not, you will be courting stiffness, chills, and possibly worse. Present manufacturing rationalization and public demand are for non-iron materials. These are fundamentally inferior to the absorbent, pure, natural cottons and wools which used to monopolize the market. So seek out clothes which possess the highest percentage of cotton or wool to man-made fibres.

Even more important is your choice of socks and shoes because your feet take a tremendous pounding during a match or practice session. No-one normally buys a pair of ill-fitting shoes but many pairs of socks are bought casually over the counter. They must be loose, absorbent, meticulously clean and ideally they should have thick, soft soles for cushioning. Some hard runners prefer two thin pairs to one thick. Comfort should govern your own choice.

Shoes must not have black soles for these mark the court surface with the same colour as the ball. That is the main reason why white clothes are customary: they offer the greatest contrast with the ball as it speeds around the court. Thick soles offer better protection but they weigh more than thin soles. Keeping comfort in mind but realising the prime importance of speed, seek flexibility, protection, and lightness in the shoes you buy. As in a motor car, your speed of movement is related to your power/weight ratio. Pay attention to traction, choosing smooth or ribbed soles according to whether you prefer a firm foothold or one which allows you to slide slightly. For me, since squash involves constant starts, stops, and turns, some kind of ribbing or dimpling seems necessary.

The swing of a squash stroke (*below*) takes a more vertical route than that of a tennis stroke, with the racket remaining nearer to the striker and so reducing the likelihood of hitting the opponent. Compare it with the more horizontal tennis stroke (*below right*), in which the racket travels farther away from the striker's body, both in the backswing and the follow-through

Preparation and Fitness

A horizontal swing back (*above left*) too easily leads to . . . a long follow-through and an injured opponent (*above*)

Undeniably, squash is a fast game but actual analysis reveals that it is not quite so fast as a casual glance might suggest, especially for the player who establishes command of any rally. Movement is then relatively slight, certainly a fraction of that of the hapless opponent being manoeuvred into all four corners of the court.

Some years ago I used five other interested observers to make a complete analysis of an open championship semi-final between Ken Hiscoe of Australia and Aftab Jawaid of Pakistan. Each of the five concentrated on measuring or assessing one special factor of the play. The results were surprising.

They showed that the average speed of movement of each man during the match was only 4·83 kilometres per hour (3mph). The average speed of the ball from hit to hit was a mere 32·19 kilometres per hour (20mph); true the ball began each journey at nearer 160·93 kilometres per hour (100mph) but, by the time it had hit a wall or two and the opponent made the next stroke, it was often travelling very slowly or was almost stationary. The major strain, or so the study appeared to prove, lay in the number of starts, stops, twists, stretches, and bends made by each player during the match. Hiscoe made close on 1,000 starts and stops – 993 to be precise – and almost 1,000 twists, bends, and stretches. That represented a great deal of work in 70 minutes, especially in the hot and humid atmosphere of London's Lansdowne Club. And these efforts were concentrated into short bursts of intense activity which drove the players into oxygen debt on several occasions.

The relevance of this to beginners and novices should be apparent. Fitness is essential. A novice playing someone of similar standard need not possess the lungs and heart of a world champion but they must be adequate to cope with the stress his or her standard of play imposes. Fortunately, lungs and heart are comparatively easy to build up. Patient jogging and running are the method. Daily doses may be boring, but extra verve and zest in everyday life and play must be worth a little purposeful effort. Just remember: always work up to top speed slowly. As for the bending and twisting, these can be developed practising by oneself. And stretching is another aspect of play which may need special attention, particularly by middle-aged people who have not exercised for many years. I strongly recommend Yoga.

Fundamentals of Stroke Technique

Squash differs from tennis and badminton, the other major racket games, in one fundamental respect. In tennis and badminton the opponents are separated from each other by the net; in squash they both occupy the entire court. Moreover, they are – or should be – running around at speed so that they are often in close proximity to one another, usually increasingly so towards the end of a match as tiredness drains away the stamina of the contestants. This physical closeness during play exercises an important influence on stroke technique generally.

It is obviously imperative that players maintain considerable racket control. If they do not, there is constant danger of an uncontrolled, wild swing severely injuring the other player's eyes, nose, or face generally. Even in international-class tournaments it is by no means unusual to see one or even both contestants ending a close, tense match with cut faces and bloodstained clothes more in keeping with boxing than a racket game.

The beautifully flowing follow-through of a Clive Lloyd at cricket or a Jimmy Connors at tennis would, if emulated on a squash court, offer a positive, ever-present danger to the other player. Consequently, effective squash strokes entail a more pronounced use of the wrist and forearm and a severely curtailed follow-through. This whipping action of wrist and forearm is particularly apparent in the forehand strokes of top-grade championship players. At its best the forehand drive is strongly reminiscent of the way children whipped spinning tops.

There are other differences inherent in the game. One is the way players constantly seek to hit the ball onto the front wall so that it rebounds into the junction of a side wall and the floor – the 'nick' – thus causing it to 'die' instantly and irretrievably.

Another is the limited value of sheer power when compared with tennis. In the latter the aim normally is to place the ball so that it speeds past your opponent. Once that has happened the player has no hope of reaching and returning it unless the pace of the shot is very slow. In squash you can hit the ball past your opponent but if it is a fast drive the player has a good chance of waiting for the ball to rebound off the back or a side wall before making a perfectly effective reply. So, much more than in tennis or badminton, there is an optimum speed for every stroke you make, but when your opponent is hustling and harrying you all over the court it is seldom easy to think analytically about such intellectual factors as the correct strength of your shot. The overwhelming tendency is to hit the ball as hard as possible and hope for the best.

Yet another difference between squash and other racket games is the relatively higher use of straight shots compared to those hit across the court. In squash, balls hit across court tend to rebound off side walls into the middle where your opponent is already positioned. Balls hit straight are more likely to hug the side walls, so imposing two pressures: one the difficulty of return, the other a danger of hitting the wall and so breaking an expensive racket.

Speed, Quickness, and Anticipation

Each stroke you make is largely conditioned by the time you have at your disposal. The more time you have, the better your chance

Top row: Incorrect stance at the 'T'. Reading from left to right, this sequence shows a player who is flat-footed, stiff bodied, and unready

Bottom row: Correct stance. Note the alert eyes, racket at the ready, and body, legs, and feet poised for action. When forced to move to the right, this player uses the left leg to turn and move. Stretching off the back leg, he can hit a ball hugging the side wall

 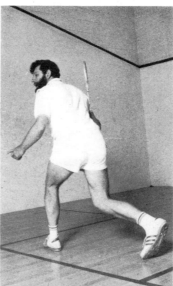 

of stroking the ball in the orthodox ways that cause it to hug the walls and floor and find the 'nick' with the greatest frequency. When forced to hurry, your instinct is to maintain the rally as best you can. So whether attacking or defending, quickness of thought, hand, and foot are primary assets. Quick movements may be yours by a divine gift but that does not liberate you from the arduousness of intensive speed training.

Understand that quickness and speed are not the same thing. Quickness is the ability to make the first, tiny movement in the smallest possible fraction of a second. Speed is the time you take to run a given distance or make a particular movement once that tiny, first step has been taken.

Quickness stems from a combination of your reaction time and your power. Power is a product of your speed and your strength relative to your weight. As in a motor car, the higher the ratio of power to weight, the quicker you are. Reaction time is a combination of divine gifts and technical know-how. Its development demands a departure from the stricture 'Always keep your eye on the ball.' Squash is a fast game in which you must move at the latest as your opponent hits the ball and ideally a moment or so earlier than that.

As a beginner you are likely to be enslaved by the angles and speed at which the ball whizzes around the court. Experience, plus the 'grooving' of your strokes, should slowly free your mind for other tasks. One of these is the consideration of your position on court. Until such time as you can 'read' your opponent's shots unerringly, there is only one spot on which to base yourself after making each shot: the 'T' in the middle of the court.

From this 'T' a quick turn and one giant stride enable you to reach either side wall so that, theoretically at least, only drop shots, near perfect lobs, and subtly paced drives that hug the side walls before dying near the back wall need force you to run at all hurriedly. It may take quite a while before your sense of angles and speed and your ability to anticipate and counter your opponent's shots will allow you to dominate rallies from the 'T' while he or she helter-skelters hither and thither in vain pursuit of your fiendish placements. But whether or not on the 'T', always adopt an alert stance, knees slightly bent, racket up and slightly forward, with your wrist relaxed for rapid action. Your weight should be lightly and evenly distributed on the balls of your feet and your brain acutely concentrated on all that is happening.

Once you have begun to think ahead of the ball – that is to judge its height, direction, and speed immediately, or even before, it leaves your opponent's racket – your reflexes will slowly help you to quicken your first movement. Later you will start to think about your opponent's play, anticipating the likeliest replies in many given situations and beginning to move into position before the ball is hit. You may get it wrong at first but if you study the later stages of this book and the game itself you should soon attain this

States of readiness: the player at the back demonstrates the correct approach, i.e. watching his opponent make his shot and thereby anticipating his own next move

attribute, which will give you more time for your own shots.

The key factor in good anticipation, however, lies in taking your eyes off the ball for momentary glimpses of your opponent's wrist, feet, legs, body, etc. because they frequently yield valuable clues about intentions before any stroke is actually made. These quick glances demand careful judgment. However, once you attain moderate proficiency you will know where most of your own shots are going almost at the moment of racket and ball impact. Your aim, say, is cross court and you meet the ball precisely with the 'sweet spot' of your racket. Even wearing a blindfold you could probably move to within a couple of feet of the line the ball will take on its return path. So now is the moment – from your crouched position on the 'T' – to look quickly and perceptively at your opponent's feet, arms, racket, and legs in order to 'read' that next shot before it is actually made. Do not worry unduly about the ball. If your sequence of looking is feet, arms, wrist, racket, the ball must return to your vision in ample time for you to follow it from the racket to the spot where you next hit it . . . unhurriedly if your clue-reading has been skilful and accurate.

Some people seem to be born with an inbuilt computing system which tells them, 'If I hit the ball there, his answer will have to be here and that will allow me to hit it there . . .' and so on. Accomplished billiards and snooker players sometimes score here for their games are essentially concerned with balls rebounding at angles. Those lacking such assets need not despair; careful study of the game backed by practice sessions in which you give full rein to imagination and the reading of the game can help enormously. As with all aspects of squash, test your ability slowly at first and put real pressure on your opponent only when you have acquired sound, basic skill in anticipation.

Chapter Two
Learning the Basic Ground Strokes

The Grip

First, how to hold the racket. Obviously, the racket itself cannot move; it must be propelled by a person or a machine. It is simply an extension of the player's arm and hand – the grip is the link. Like a chain, the whole lever of arm and racket is only as strong as its weakest link – a point which cannot be overstressed. Research carried out on world-class tennis players shows that the actual velocity of a ball leaving the racket can be halved if the racket is held limply. However, there is that basic difference in technique brought about by the need to control the follow-through in squash. It imposes the requirement to whip the racket head rather than swing it, and whipping demands ample flexibility of wrist.

So to the grip you should adopt. Hold your racket by its throat out in front of you, the strings perpendicular to the ground. Adjust it, if necessary, so that you cannot see the strings, only the outer edge of the frame. Now shake hands with the handle. The 'V' formed by your forefinger and thumb should be centred on an imaginary line running from the edge of the frame; you should not be able to see the strings. The end of the handle, the butt, should project only fractionally out of your hand, no more than half an inch. Your second, third, and fourth fingers should grip the handle firmly but not as though you are trying to squeeze it like an orange. Such overtense squeezing causes tiredness and reduces wrist flexibility.

Now to the forefinger and thumb. First try keeping your forefinger actually touching your second finger and wrap your thumb around the handle so that it overlaps your forefinger. If you then grip tightly, you will feel tension in the 'V' of your thumb and forefinger. Now let the forefinger move slightly up the handle until all tension vanishes. Repeat this procedure with your thumb, which should neither be wrapped tightly around the handle nor lie straight along it. Instead, it should be moved until it lies partially around the handle so that you obtain maximum 'feel' in your forefinger and thumb, and the basic strength of your grip rests in your second, third, and fourth fingers. Let your wrist relax while you gently shake the racket around.

On court fast returns will hammer into your racket strings and you need strength to counter the impact while developing your own power. Yet you must continue to use your racket with the sensitivity of a violinist rather than the brute force of a carpenter driving a heavy nail into a wall. Naturally, the degree of sensitivity

varies according to whether you are hitting a full-blooded drive or caressing the ball into a junction of front and side wall in a court-opening drop shot. Yet the basic consideration remains unchanged. Your grip is the link between the ball and the part of your brain which computes the sensations of touch. Only if your brain receives the maximum supply of touch sensations can it provide the optimum instructions to your racket-governing muscles.

That grip should suffice for every stroke you make, your wrist position bringing about the variations of racket angle necessary for forehand and backhand returns. Hold your arm and racket straight out in front of you with the racket handle parallel to the ground and the racket face at right angles to it. Turn your wrist and racket slightly clockwise so that the left side of the racket face points upwards just a little; the 'V' of your thumb and forefinger should point towards the ceiling. This gives the angle for forehand drives, those strokes which are made on the right-hand side of a right-handed player with the fore, or front, part of the lower arm facing the ball during the execution of the stroke. Now rotate the wrist and racket anti-clockwise until the right side of the racket face is tilted slightly upwards. That is the angle for backhands, shots hit with the back of your arm towards the ball and made on the left-hand side of right-handed players.

A final reminder: always grip your racket firmly and keep your wrist flexible so that you can whip – or slash – your strokes. Some players find it necessary to hold their rackets slightly closer to the racket head so that an inch or so of handle peeps out at the bottom. This inhibits power and should be adopted only if you decide after a prolonged trial that you simply cannot control the ball when holding your racket at the end of its handle.

Top row: Cocking the wrist for forehand and backhand. Looking at the forehand first, the player on the left gets it right. His cocked wrist enables the racket head to be whipped into the stroke, thus increasing the speed of shot enormously. In the backhand shot, it's the stance and cocked wrist of the player on the right which enables body pivot and wrist whip to double the speed of the swing

Centre row: The longer your stroke maintains ball-racket contact, the more you 'feel' the ball and so the better you should be able to control it. This beautifully controlled stroke has held the ball on the strings to the limits of possibility

Stroke Technique

I said earlier that touch is a product of time: the longer the ball stays on the racket strings, the greater will be the number of electrical impulses transmitted from the fingers and hand to the brain. Power, however, results from a number of factors. The more you can increase the speed of the racket head at the moment of impact relative to the weight of the racket, the greater will be the speed of the ball leaving the racket.

Racket manufacturers are now altering the ratios of weight distribution so that some rackets have more weight in the head, although handling like lighter-headed equipment in dynamic situations, but increases in racket-head speed were already obtainable through improved stroke technique.

There are, in fact, four ways in which speed has always been imparted to the effective pace of a racket head. The actual swing of your arm during the stroke gives the basic speed; let's call it 'b'. Snapping your wrist and, to some degree, your elbows adds additional speed, 'c'. Rotation of your body in the direction of your stroke adds still more speed, 'd', and finally any forward run adds yet more speed, 'e'. So the speed at which the ball leaves the racket is the sum of $b + c + d + e$.

There is one final theoretical point to bear in mind concerning the basic strokes. You should always try to keep the ball low and skidding when forcing the pace. Failure to do so results in the ball rebounding off a side or back wall so that your opponent has ample time to counter with a stroke at least as aggressive as the one you have just made. The right amount of undercut or slice – that is a mixture of under- and sidespin – helps to make the ball skid rather than lift after bouncing. However, do not overestimate either the amount of spin you should impart or the extent to which it will make the ball 'die' after bouncing. Exaggerations of spin

Bottom row: The swing of the striker's arm (*b*) and wrist snap (*c*), plus his body pivot (*d*) and forward movement (*e*), all combine to give a racket-head velocity (*v*) which can be expressed thus: $v = b + c + d + e$. In plain language, that means a mighty fast shot, much faster than could result from a mere swing of the arm

slow the ball and counteract the effects you should be trying to achieve.

The three requirements, then, when hitting basic, after the ball has bounced, strokes are:

1 extended ball-racket contact time,
2 maximum racket-head velocity, and
3 slight undercut.

All other factors, like footwork, body turn, type of swing and so on, are important only in so far as they assist those primary requirements. How, then, can this be ensured without creating inhibitions through overdoses of complicated technical instructions? Firstly, by keeping firmly in mind the supreme importance of that fraction of the total swing, the 152 millimetres (6 inches) before and after impact, the so-called 'zip area', and secondly, by moving smoothly and rhythmically to the ball whenever possible.

Footwork

Your footwork should always be so directed that those four racket-head speed factors are all at maximum effectiveness when your racket impacts the ball. Timing is critical at this moment and timing is tremendously dependent on correct footwork. You're progressing when you can judge your opponent's shot and dance lightly to the side of the ball. When you can do so in a firm yet relaxed manner that permits body turn, etc., you're really getting places. This means giving yourself as much time as you can, bearing in mind that your opponent will be striving constantly to harry and hustle you. Early preparation is important to consistency in stroke making. If you have to scamper for the ball, scamper with your racket at the ready.

Drop shots followed by lofted returns – or 'lobs' – deep into one or the other corner are a routine in common use so how best to cover the court when forced into a defensive role? Firstly, be clear that on some occasions there will be no question of dancing lightly and stylishly into position to execute a flowing, textbook demonstration of how to play squash. Yours will be a frantic gallop followed by a desperate lunge made in the hope of keeping the ball in play. Although you must never become complacent, at least take comfort in the thought that the more successful 'scrape-back lunges' you make, the harder you are probably trying. And the harder you try, the quicker you are likely to become, so that your ratio of well-controlled strokes to those made under duress should gradually increase.

That much thoroughly understood, consider now how to move on a squash court. Problem number one is that there is another player – and racket – occupying the space in which you operate and all too often that person will seem to be between you and the ball. Furthermore, after making your stroke you must move out of the way so that he or she can have an unimpeded swing at the ball.

Bearing in mind the limited period of time between each shot, one is led to the inevitable conclusion that the best movements are

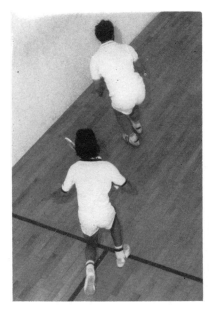

more akin to dancing than track running. The prime need is to be able to start, stop, turn, twist, and bend. So during each rally keep your knees slightly bent, your weight lightly and evenly poised on the balls of your feet, and those feet moving slightly so that inertia is reduced to a minimum and you can dart immediately in any direction. This perpetual movement approach to footwork demands physical and mental effort but that expenditure will be more than compensated for by the greater ease with which you will be able to reach your opponent's best placements. As in so many facets of sport, you should constantly be balancing one factor against another and choosing the more profitable.

Fundamentally, squash is a sideways game. Frequently strokes are taught with the feet so placed that a continuation of the line running through the two ankles would momentarily follow the direction of the hit. In such instances, post-impact movement is, of course, necessary to maintain balance. In match situations such precision is seldom achieved, though championship-standard players hit a high proportion of shots with their foot positions approximating to the ideal. In my analyses of top-class players in action approximately 34% of strokes were found to be made with textbook footwork. The other 66% were struck with the feet in various facing-the-wall positions. In most cases, body and hip rotation achieved the desired sideways-to-the-ball swing of the racket.

For power and accuracy the feet should be fairly widely spread, say 76 or 101 millimetres (3 or 4 inches) wider than the shoulders. A correctly taken stroke will leave your weight on your front foot. It should transfer from back to front foot as your free shoulder pivots with the hit. Theoretically, your front foot should be firmly in place just ahead of the actual hit but Newton's law about bodies in motion maintaining that state until a force bears on them

23

Above: To obtain maximum power and racket-head control on a forehand, turn sideways to the direction in which you intend hitting the ball, using body pivot and textbook, 'foot-across' footwork. An analysis of match play shows that only one in three shots is struck with the front foot across but 95% have the necessary body pivot

Below: Sideways for a backhand too. The swing's follow-through takes the racket away from the body so it is more necessary to move the front leg across to accentuate body pivot away from the ball and then into the hit

applies to all ball-and-bat games. Providing your run is smooth and controlled, you are as stable when moving as when your feet are planted. Additionally, when moving you are better able to sway one way or another if the ball behaves unexpectedly. This smoothness of movement and stroke can be practised alone on a court to acquire the basic technique. It will then develop under match-play conditions. After making your stroke, use the foot which is not carrying any weight to take a big step towards the position you wish to reach, normally the 'T'. The next big step by what was the front foot should take you onto that 'T'.

To get the feel of all this, take your racket and stand facing a wall about a metre (3 feet 3 inches) away from it, feet spaced slightly outside the width of your shoulders. Extend your arm and racket full out to the side, bending your elbow and cocking your wrist so that the racket shaft is pointing to the ceiling with the racket strings facing the wall. Swing your arm and racket as if hitting a ball in front of your knees and snap your wrist back to a

straight position to give the racket head greater speed. Finish the
swing round your forward hip. Use your free arm first to turn your
hitting shoulder away from the imaginary, approaching ball, then
to assist it by swinging with the stroke. Let your weight transfer
from back to front foot in time with your swing. Though it may
seem somewhat unnatural, move the weightless foot as soon as
you have completed your imaginary stroke. You'll probably need to
put in some practice on this method of recovering position. When
back at the 'T', keep bouncing slightly and lightly to minimize the
effects of body inertia and do not let your mental alertness sag.

No matter how eager your body may be, it must receive instructions from your brain before it can move effectively. So quick
footwork is as much mental as it is physical. One vital reminder:
your knees play an important part in alert movement so be sure
they are slightly bent at all times.

Knees were made for
bending, so emulate the
player on the right when
a low ball skids through

The player on the left executes a textbook forehand drive. Contrast his swing with that of his novice opponent

The Forehand

Now put all that theory into practice by studying the forehand. Imagine a stroke made when the ball comes to you a couple of feet or so above floor level at a comfortable pace on your right. As soon as you realise the depth and direction of the oncoming ball, you turn to face the wall with your feet slightly farther apart than your shoulder width, say by 76 or 101 millimetres (3 or 4 inches). Cock your wrist upwards as you might when hammering a nail into a wall. Swing your arm sideways from the shoulder with your elbow bent so that your hand nears your right shoulder. Simultaneously turn your body to the right, dropping your left shoulder and raising your right, so that the back of your left shoulder is slightly towards the ball. When it comes within hitting distance, uncock your arm and wrist as you whip the racket at the ball, your body pivoting strongly to add speed to the racket head, which continues to whip round your left side after impact so minimizing the chances of wounding your opponent. The hitting point should be around 305 to 457 millimetres (12 to 18 inches) away from your body and just in front of your forward (i.e. left) leg.

26

Time your swing and pivot to reach maximum speed at the moment of impact. The tempo should be slow-fast rather than the fast-slow slashes prevalent among unthinking beginners and novices. Your racket should whip slightly under the ball; not so that the shot is lofted, but enough to impart a slight underspin to it. Keep your head down and your eyes looking at the point in space where you hit the ball until a moment after impact. Lifting the head too soon is probably the commonest fault in all ball games and is frequently a result of over-anxiety – the hitter is so scared of missing, maybe subconsciously, that he or she looks up ahead of the hit to see if the ball is really going where it was aimed.

Concentrate furiously on the 'zip area' (see page 22) and let the follow-through of the entire stroke flow naturally out of the thrust you develop with body, arm, and wrist when the racket head whips through it.

The right and wrong way to hit a backhand. Notice particularly how the player on the right develops maximum body-turn through good footwork, and top racket-head velocity through wrist snap

The Backhand
This real need for maximum thrust through the zip area applies equally to shots hit on the backhand when, usually, you will be facing the left-hand wall with your right shoulder pointing to the

front wall. In the forehand, the backswing takes your racket away from your body and the follow-through across it. In the backhand, your backswing is round your body and the follow-through away from it. This increases the ease with which you can make your racket head 'stay with the ball' after impact, so improving touch and assisting power. Hence the greater security of most backhands, even if they may lack the breathtaking speed of many forehands.

The backhand is, in fact, a more natural swing than the forehand. Think how you deal a pack of cards or toss your hat into a chair. That is the basic arm movement. Now to convert it into a squash stroke.

First, the feet should be slightly farther apart than your shoulders, with the front foot slightly nearer to the side wall than the back foot. The object is to give you a firm, steady base for your stroke; after all, the guns on a battleship are heavily bolted to the deck. Grip your racket firmly and with your wrist cocked upwards. Letting it hang down loosely results in weakness, poor control, and even pain when the opponent's shot is hard.

So, with your feet firmly positioned and your arm and wrist well braced, swing your racket backwards so that its head goes above and slightly behind your left shoulder. That shoulder should be raised just a little so that your right shoulder is down and pointing at the ball as it comes towards you, almost as if it were turning to maintain its 'sighting' of the ball. Judge the unwinding of your body to the right and the swing of your racket so that you strike the ball just a little ahead of your right leg.

Uncock your forearm and snap your wrist to add to overall racket velocity, letting the strings slide fractionally under the ball in order to apply slight underspin. Pivot your shoulder in harmony with your racket swing to add power but do not let your racket travel too far after the ball as that endangers your opponent. Your follow-through, though vigorous, should be round your right side and close to your body, so reducing the likelihood of clouting your opponent as well as the ball.

Many players lock their wrists when hitting the ball backhanded, claiming that it helps control. Maybe they are right but the relationship between control and power depends on the overall personality of the player ('personality' being a more embracing term than the usual 'character') and you will automatically perform in keeping with your basic personality. My recommendation is that you should always be striving intelligently for greater power when practising or playing those whom you can beat comfortably. That way you will slowly raise your basic power without sacrificing control.

So what about that use of your wrist? Hold your right arm in front of you with your forearm parallel to the ground and the 'V' between your thumb and first finger pointing at your nose. Now move your hand to left and right, using your wrist as if it were the

hinge of a door. This demonstrates how much extra racket-head speed you should be able to develop if you learn to incorporate this wrist action into your stroke. That extra racket-head speed spells more power which, in turn, means more points won. When next you play, consider in advance this problem of control versus power and resolve gradually to increase the latter without any decrease of the former.

The right and wrong way to achieve wrist snap and body pivot. Note how the man at the back moves his left foot over and cocks his wrist upwards

Of course, this involves more than merely increasing the use of your wrist in stroke-making. It means making full use of body pivot and arm swing and so harmonizing body, arm, and wrist that all reach top speed at the precise moment your racket strikes the ball. To repeat, your racket can actually govern the ball only during that fraction of a second they are in contact. Actually the moment is generally no longer than 0·005 of a second. Double that figure for softly struck drop shots but it is still a minuscule moment. So for maximum effect every detail of your stroke must be impeccably timed to harmonize.

This entails freedom of swing and you know without me telling you the arch enemy of freedom of movement; it is tension. Tense muscles lose their elasticity, and elasticity produces speed. So maintain concentration in your mind but let your muscles relax. They should not be 'sloppy' – just relaxed to the degree that will let you move them sweetly and quickly.

Avoid 'muscling' the ball or slashing wildly at it because both usually result in the racket reaching top speed before impact and decelerating at the actual moment of the hit. In a nutshell, swing your racket and let it, rather than your muscles, do the work. Two or three perfectly timed strokes on court will give you the feeling far better than any words. There is a sweet effortlessness and vivid speed about a perfectly harmonized and correctly timed stroke with any implement, be it a racket, cricket bat, hockey stick, or the like. Once you experience that sensation, try to let it seep deep into your

Handling a low ball. The player in the lower picture gets it right, getting down to the ball by moving the left leg first, bending the knee, and taking the eyes near to the racket face to ensure better visibility and greater freedom from parallax. Balance also tends to be better. The other player makes the mistake of reaching for the ball. With his eyes far from the racket face, the chances of errors caused by parallax are increased

consciousness so that you can recapture it ever more frequently.

That relaxation must spread to your legs and knees. You will have to hit many balls that do not rise much above the floor. Get down to them by bending your knees, taking your nose as near to the ball as is consistent with your natural swing, and try to keep the shaft of your racket at least parallel with the ground.

Practice Pointers

Now just a few reminders before leaving the subject of how to make your basic strokes. Ensure that you follow through close to your body so that you do not hit your opponent with your racket. Once you have hit the ball, give your opponent room to reach it but in doing so make for the 'T' of the court. After hitting the ball, make that first movement towards the 'T' with a goodly stride with your back foot; there isn't time to rock back onto it before moving the front leg. With footwork as a whole, avoid being dogmatic, especially over the 'front foot across' rule. There are times when that front leg and foot position is impractical or restrictive. In such cases, compensate with body pivot or sway. Concentrate on maximum zip-area effectiveness and all else should follow naturally.

Chapter Three
Volleying

The Volley

Strokes made before the ball bounces are named 'volleys' and they possess one major, inherent advantage. They give your opponent less time to recover from his or her previous shot and make another. Simple reckoning can emphasize this point. Take a ball travelling the full length of a side wall. If you return it from the back wall after it has bounced, it covers 9·75 metres (32 feet) from the front wall to your hit. If you move up to the service line to volley the ball, you save 8·53 metres (28 feet) – the extra 4·26 metres (14 feet) it would have travelled to the back wall plus the first 4·26 metres it would have travelled after you hit it. That represents a lot of 'hustle' for your opponent. But it means quite a bit for you too: if you choose to volley the ball, you also have less time for your own stroke. So volleying is mainly for the quick and the adventurous . . . and those who enjoy exploiting those qualities, even if they are not especially endowed with them.

Fundamentally the actual strokes used in volleying do not differ from the basic forehand and backhand but there is an even greater necessity for you to keep your nose near to the ball. Do not take this too literally but, nevertheless, remember the importance of bending your knees to the low volleys and of keeping your back down too. The nearer your eyes are to the line of the oncoming ball, the less are the chances of miss-hits through parallax: your racket face and eyes will be 'looking' along the same line and not at differing angles to it.

Hitting the ball before it bounces, or volleying, hustles an opponent but it demands quickness and a slightly different stroke technique: the racket face must line up with the incoming ball early and positively so that it can be punched firmly onto the wall. Here the player takes a forehand volley

In this backhand volley the ball has travelled straight but is being hit at an angle. This time the racket face is not lined up with the approaching ball. Such changes of direction demand meticulous timing

As with ground strokes, volleys should be made with the arm comfortably crooked and the wrist cocked so that it may be snapped into the hit for extra racket-head velocity and power. The one exception is when you are forced to make your stroke at full stretch. So be it. Any arm bend will be out of the question but realise that you are making your stroke under duress and mentally resolve that you will not lightly permit yourself to be so out-manoeuvred again.

When you rob an opponent of time you put him or her under extra pressure. So mix the pace and direction of your volleys. Play some at full power down the side wall, others across the court; use reverse angles, drop shots, and occasional lobs (more of all these later). All must be hit with a firm grip and purposeful mind. There is no place for drawing back when volleying.

The one exception is when you are up court and your opponent hits a full-blooded drive which you reply to with a volley which drops short near the side wall before, you intend, dying in the nick between floor and wall. Then you must take speed off the ball, perhaps by letting it merely hit your racket strings without moving the racket, maybe even by drawing your racket back slightly at the moment the ball hits the strings. In either case, think clearly and purposefully. Grip your racket firmly and brace your forearm as you play the ball. On no account let your grip, wrist, or arm go limp. The drop volley may be a soft stroke but it is an aggressive one and, as such, must be made with strong purpose.

The Half Volley

Now, apart from ground strokes and volleys, there is one other point at which your racket can meet the ball and that is at the

moment it actually bounces. Such shots are called 'half volleys'. Because your racket will be between your eyes and the ball there is not quite the imperative need to crouch low. You may drop the head of your racket below the level of your wrist, providing you maintain complete control of it and the ball pitches near to your feet. If the ball is wide of you and you attempt a stroke you are, in cricketing terms, committing the sin of leaving a gap between bat and pad. You may not be able to see the actual hit when you half volley but that does not eliminate the need to keep eyes and ball on as near as possible the same line.

More Practice Pointers

You now have an inkling of the differing ways in which you can hit the ball. Go on court alone and familiarize yourself with the way you move and the sense of hitting a stroke correctly. Many strokes feel good but when you make one which is timed exactly to the correct two-hundredth part of a second and with every segment of your swing and body weight travelling along the line of the hit that good feeling is magnified a thousand-fold.

When practising alone, concentrate on smoothness and rhythm, moving ever more widely and quickly as the actual mechanics of hitting gradually become 'grooved'. Mix such practice with sessions against an opponent or fellow improver. Even though you may be under pressure, strive for smoothness and rhythm. Then, when you start to play games and score, forget about technique and strive to win the points. Trust your body to repeat the movements you have practised under no-pressure situations and concentrate all your mental and physical energies on winning, since winning can become habitual.

Chapter Four
Serving

Every rally begins with a service and as you can only score points when you are 'hand-in' or serving it is, clearly, an extremely important shot. It differs only in one basic way from other strokes you make: you begin with the ball in your hand instead of it coming your way after your opponent has hit it.

Tennis abounds with unreturnable services; squash does not. Yet this is no signal to treat the service merely as a way of starting the rally. Sheer speed may possess only marginal advantages but variations of pace, direction, and, less frequently, length can, if used thoughtfully and with good control, establish an attacking position in a majority of rallies. Conversely, a badly directed, poor-length service against an alert, aggressive opponent will frequently cost you the point immediately.

The rules are clear. You must have one foot inside the lines which form the service box – note inside, not on the lines – and the ball must hit the front wall above the cut line. Again, the ball must be above the line, not on or below it.

If allowed to bounce, the served ball must fall within your opponent's half-court, including the service box. However, the receiver can choose to play a fault. If your first service is faulty, you are allowed a second chance. If that is also a fault, your opponent becomes 'hand-in' and can now score points while you become 'hand-out' and must recapture 'hand-in' before you can score again.

Within these limitations you have an advantage as hand-in so use it wisely. Think how and where you will direct the ball before taking up position. And relax. Once in position, imagine vividly

Below: The forehand serve. One foot remains in the service box until the ball has left the racket. Eyes must stay on the ball and there must be no jerking up of the head and shoulders to check where the ball should go before it is hit. Note how the racket face is tilted in the second and third pictures to impart slice and lift

Opposite bottom: The forehand serve from the left-hand court. The ball travels towards the right side wall and, therefore, towards the opponent's forehand. Great care is needed to ensure its altitude and direction do not offer a set-up which can be killed. Hence the meticulous way the server is watching the ball and controlling his swing

the service you are about to project and, with that picture in mind, repeat it with racket and ball.

The 'bread-and-butter' service is one which clears the short line, slides off the side wall, and then dies in the back corner of the opponent's half court; see Diagram 2 on page 36. Unvarying repetition of this tactic would be unwise since any alert, eager opponent will quickly begin moving forward to volley the ball before it reaches the short-line area.

A shrewd mixture of serves in which the ball is lobbed high and deep should inhibit an opponent from automatically leaping forward every time you serve. To produce this effect you need to hit the ball about 2·44 metres (8 feet) above the cut line, taking care that it does not bounce from there onto the side wall above the out-of-court line. Strive to keep the ball near the side wall and get as much length as you can without letting it hit the back wall before it bounces on the floor. When the ball hits the back wall before the floor, it bounds more easily for your opponent than

The backhand serve is used infrequently. Because impact occurs near the half-court line, the ball can be made to hug the side wall more closely than is possible with a forehand service. However, much practice is necessary

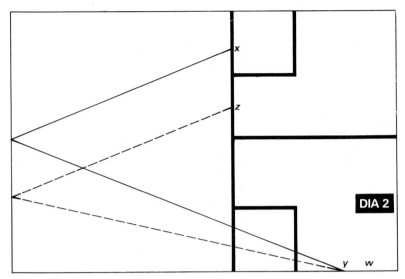

Diagram 2: The 'bread-and-butter' service. *x* to *y* is a forehand service, *z* to *y* a backhand service to the same length. Note that the ball travels nearer to the wall when it crosses the short line on the backhand service. Aim for *w* with a high lob serve. To practise good-length serving, put a box 305 to 457 millimetres (12 to 18 inches) long and 229 millimetres (9 inches) wide at point *w* and try lobbing a ball into it from just left of the 'T'. Serve fifty times, varying your height from time to time, and note how many lobs drop directly into the box. Next time you play, repeat the exercise and compare results

when the reverse occurs. If you can consistently lob within 0·61 metres (2 feet) of the back wall, you will not come to a great deal of harm.

There are two ways of making both a bread-and-butter and a lob serve. One is to drop the ball and hit it with an underarm motion as if lofting it for a child to catch; the other is with a sideways hit which you begin by throwing the ball towards the side wall at shoulder height. 'Throwing the ball' is perhaps too imprecise a description. When serving, whether fast, slow, underarm, sidearm or overhead, take great care in placing the ball exactly where you will be able to make perfect contact at the correct moment of impact. This will help you to develop the unhurried, rhythmic swing necessary for the unvarying accuracy which keeps the receiver guessing and on the defensive.

Think first of the length for which you are striving, then the distance from ceiling and side wall of the place on the front wall you must hit with the ball, and finally of the strength of hit needed. Fix all in your mind before actually serving. If you must err in direction, tend towards the middle line rather than the side wall; a service which bounces off the side wall before it reaches an alert receiver is simply begging to be hit aggressively. So also does one that is too near the middle, but not quite to the same extent as one off the wall. Best practise, however, until you can attain the height, direction, length, and speed you desire every time you hit the ball.

The alternative to the lob or bread-and-butter services is the straightforward serve hit overarm, as in tennis, either to the junction of base and side walls or aimed for the middle line dividing the two half-courts. No matter what type of service you deliver, automatically make for the "l" immediately afterwards. But, remember, if you try a surprise serve down the middle line, make sure you give your opponent room to make a return stroke.

When serving, the nearer your racket is to the middle line when you hit the ball the better will be your chances of sliding it down the side wall. Theoretically, this means that when serving from the right-hand half-court you should start with your right foot in the box and your left as near to the centre line as you can comfortably manage, while leaning as far to the middle as you can before hitting the ball with a backhand stroke. Since this is not easy, you will have to compute for yourself the advantages it offers relative to the better control you should be able to show when serving with a forehand stroke made with your right foot in the service box but your left foot forward in the forecourt rather than towards the middle. Practise both types of service often and intelligently so that you can produce long or short, fast or slow, forehand or backhand with equal facility.

Your object should normally be surprise, although there may be occasions when your opponent lacks the ability to cope with real power. However, in that situation you are likely to be so superior that you can win no matter what method of serving you adopt. Remember with all power serves that, if left, the ball will probably rebound off the back wall and so be relatively simple for your opponent to hit, in all probability with considerable aggression. Occasionally you may win the point outright with a serve but the likelier pattern is 'good serve, weak reply; aggressive shot, weaker reply; extremely aggressive shot . . .' and so on. So learn a variety of different serves and practise all of them so that you can establish your superiority at the start of each rally.

Spin

You can affect the way the ball rebounds from the front and side walls by the application of spin. Virtually every hit you make must put some spin on the ball, be it very little. During service, such natural spin will be killed by the energy-sapping contact of ball and front wall. To sustain the spin after hitting the front wall demands extra effort. But you can learn to make the ball skid, bound, break, or mix such characteristics according to your own dictates.

Underspin causes the ball to bounce downwards off the front wall, topspin to bound upwards. Sidespin causes the ball to veer from left to right or vice versa, according to the direction in which the racket strings drag across the ball. Diagrams 3 and 4 on page 38 show how top- and underspin affect performance. Replace 'floor' with 'side wall' and work out for yourself how sidespin affects the path of the ball.

The application of spin is not limited to serving. Use it at all times but never let it become your master. Spin is a good servant used sparingly and judiciously but it can become addictive and so work to your opponent's advantage. Refer again to the section dealing with the fundamentals of ground strokes (page 22) to refresh your memory on the importance of the zip area in a total stroke. The maximum extension of ball-racket contact time was

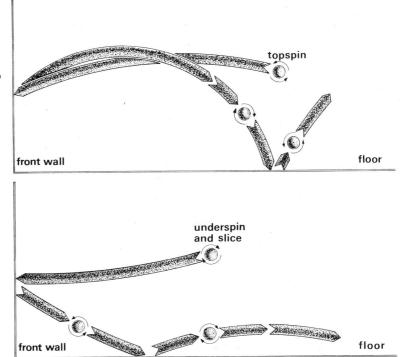

Diagram 3: Apply topspin to a drive and you make the top of the ball rotate towards the wall like a turning wheel. But spin is reversed by contact with a surface so the ball 'kicks' upwards after hitting the front wall, adding length to the path it takes before bouncing. There, again, the spin is reversed, making the ball bound upwards

Diagram 4: Underspin causes the underside of the ball to rotate towards the wall. The spin is reversed at contact, making the ball 'kick' downwards and reducing the length of its path before bouncing. It is again reversed on contact with the floor, and this causes the ball to skid forward with some acceleration.

For the sake of clarity, the effects have been somewhat exaggerated in these diagrams.

shown to be vital. Since sliding the racket over, under or sideways on the ball will extend that time somewhat, spin can be said to aid control. But as the racket should travel at an angle relative to the direction you wish the ball to take, there must be some loss of power in the application of spin.

Excessive spin demands longer ball-racket contact time but the theoretical advantage thus gained is diminished by the difference between the path of your racket and that of the ball after it leaves your racket. So, as in all things, moderation is the norm for which you should strive, leaving excesses for desperate retrieves or for experimenting under no-pressure, practice situations.

Top- or underspin revolves the ball on its vertical axis, sidespin on its horizontal axis. Yet the word one hears most frequently in this context is 'slice'. There is nothing mysterious about this. Slice merely causes the ball to spin somewhere between those vertical and horizontal axes, exactly where depending on the degree of slice you choose to apply. Since slice mixes the effects of the two fundamental spins, it can cause the ball to behave in a variety of ways . . . including hugging the wall even when it approaches at a tangent.

To learn the different effects of all these spins, go on court alone and practise applying over-, under-, and sidespins, as well as various types of slice. Use extreme spins at first and then, when you understand clearly their full effects, cut out the excesses and try different types of slice. An hour's correct practice will teach you quicker than any further words I could write.

Chapter Five
Rallying

Once the service is delivered, the rally gets under way, beginning, of course, with the return of service. This is a specialized shot but it would be best for the moment to leave discussion of it until the various options which occur in rallies have been studied.

These fall into six main categories:
1 the down-the-wall shot,
2 the drop shot,
3 the lob,
4 the angle,
5 the reverse angle, and
6 the boast.

Incidentally, that order is merely for convenience and is in no way related to relative importance.

Using Height, Length and Direction

Before I go on to describe those options, consider for a moment the function of the rally. Both players should be seeking the "T" as a base; both should be manoeuvring for a weak return which can be demolished.

Now take up your ideal position on the 'T' of a squash court. Make a lunge to the left and stretch your racket towards the side wall. Repeat this exercise to the right. You can cover virtually the entire width of a squash court with one stride and a stretched-out racket in either direction. Those side walls are 6·40 metres (21 feet) apart. The full length of the court is 3·35 metres (11 feet) more than that: 9·75 metres (32 feet) to be precise. Consider another dimension – that from the top line on the front wall to the back wall and floor nick. It measures 10·74 metres (35 feet 4 inches). The inference should be obvious. If you want to make an opponent run as much as possible, skilled use of height and length must be more effective than merely striving for side-wall to side-wall placements.

Of course, if you make an accurate placement to one or other of those walls and then volley the return, you can make your opponent believe that the court is far wider than 6·40 metres (21 feet). On the other hand, slight inaccuracies in such placements can offer a wonderful attacking position and you will be on the receiving end of drives which force you to hurry and stretch sideways. Recall for a moment the match analysis described on page 13, which showed how stopping, starting, twisting, and bending are the prime causes of fatigue. Now, perhaps, you can understand why great champions like Geoff Hunt make such extensive use of varying height, pace, angle, and length. It would be totally wrong to allege that players do this solely to protect themselves from attack; they are far too positive in their thinking ever to act in such a negative way.

Their method of protection is attack. By moving opponents up court, then back, then sideways, then back, then forwards and so on, they force continual movement and, in so doing, increase their chances of teasing a slightly inaccurate return which can be killed. This was especially noticeable in the 1977 Lucas British Open Championship final in which Hunt beat his fellow Australian, the left-handed Cam Nancarrow. Nancarrow is lithe and naturally gifted with ball sense and good timing but it is doubtful if his studies of the game have equalled Hunt's. So it was Hunt, seemingly, who directed every shot as much with his brain as with his arm whereas Nancarrow appeared to rely on instinct more than sequential geometry. Possibly this stemmed from Hunt's early days when he was so superior to all readily available opposition in Australia that the loss of just one point in an entire match was by no means rare. And when this did happen he and his father would probe and analyse in great detail just why he lost that point . . . and then practise assiduously to safeguard against any repetitions.

To recap, then, maintaining good length is immensely important when manoeuvring for a weak return; Diagram 5 confirms this point. And another valuable objective is to try directing or angling your shots so that the ball is always travelling away from your opponent. Correct pace has a part to play here. Too slow a drive will be easy to chase. Too fast a drive may let the ball rebound off one or other of the walls back towards the centre of the court. Diagram 6 demonstrates how a shot hit in the right direction but too strongly can neutralize your objective. The optimum speed is that which prevents direct interception of the ball yet does not allow your opponent to wait until it comes off side and/or back wall towards the centre of the court. This nicety of power may be difficult to achieve under the high-speed, stressful conditions of match play, yet you should strive to develop it, especially in practice sessions.

Angled shots can be used in a variety of situations. First, if you sense your opponent has started to move in one direction, you can change the direction of your return and wrong foot him or her. Second, in a series of down-the-wall drives and lobs, the ball may come to you far enough away from the side wall to offer the choice of maintaining the down-the-wall sequence or opening up the game. This you can do by hitting the ball onto the front wall so that it bounces towards the junction of the back and side walls. Third, when your patience, skill, or sheer luck has presented you with a sitter in mid-court, you can clobber the ball hard onto the front wall so that it bounds back into the nick at one or other of the side walls. And fourth, an angled shot can also be effective when the ball is so well flighted that it cannot safely be hit until it has bounced off the side and/or back wall.

Diagrams 7 to 9 on page 42–3 illustrate some of the occasions

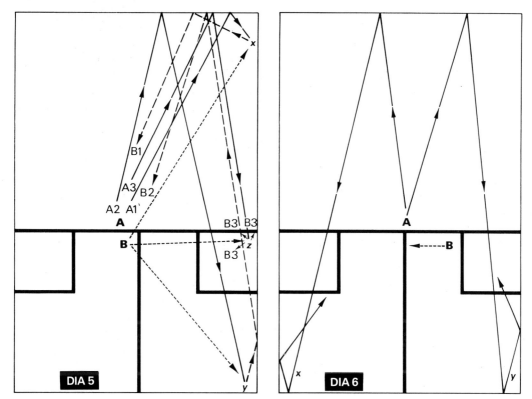

when an angled return could win the point: the circle drawn round the 'T' indicates the area of court you can cover with one big stride and a stretched racket. But, as always, never lapse into unthinking repetition. The essence of good tactics is surprise, and subtle changes of length and pace are important factors in maintaining that surprise element. Note the word 'subtle' too; if your changes are pronounced, an alert opponent can easily read them and the surprise is lost.

Down-the-Wall Shots

These are the bread-and-butter shots of the game. Their effectiveness depends to some degree on your position when you hit the ball. If you are close to the wall, you can make the ball hug it all the way up and down the court. If you are nearer the middle of the court, the ball must make an angle with the side wall and an imprecisely directed shot will result in the ball bouncing off the side wall in front of your opponent, offering the chance to win the point with a fast, nick-seeking cross-court drive – to either front corner if the ball bounces too far out. So the closer you are to the middle of the court, the more accurate you must be with the length of your down-the-wall attempt. If you must err, it is better to be overlong so that, at worst, the ball hits the side wall behind your opponent's position. True, he or she may hurry forward to play an aggressive volley but the chances are that this will not be quite so deadly as the return which could be made by letting the ball bounce, even though there would then be more time to get set.

Diagram 5: The importance of good length. If A plays a drop shot (A1), which B reaches hurriedly at *x*, B will almost certainly be forced to hook the ball onto the front wall, sending it to mid-court (B1). If A plays deep (A2) so that B must take the ball at *y*, B will be forced to boast onto the side wall, probably presenting A with another easy shot in mid-court (B2). However, if A makes a poor-length return to *z* (A3), B will be able to move easily to the ball and choose any of about eight possible shots (B3)

Diagram 6: Judging the power of a stroke. B has returned the ball and is moving to the 'T'. If A hits the ball for *x* or *y*, it will be moving away from B. If A hits too hard, however, B will be able to wait for the ball to come off the back wall. A lob to *x* or *y* is possibly the best shot

41

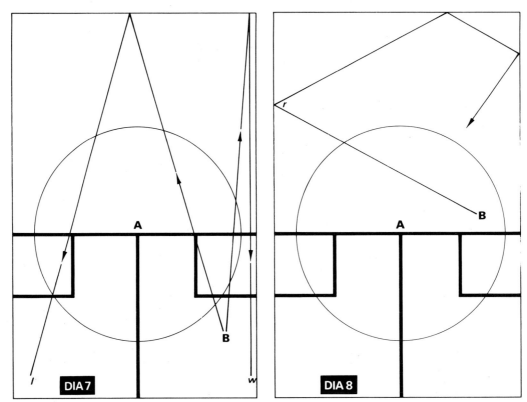

DIA 7

DIA 8

Diagrams 7–9: Angled returns. In all three diagrams, the circle indicates the area which can be covered with one big stride and a stretched racket

If B is behind A (*Diagram 7*), he or she must either lob for *l* or temporize with a wall-hugging drive or lob to *w*

If A returns the ball short (*Diagram 8*) or in such a way that B can move forward to drive or volley in front of the service box, then B can hit the ball across court in a reverse angle to *r*. Apart from forcing A to leave the 'T', this shot also causes the ball to travel rapidly near to and across A's line of vision, making it difficult to follow

If B is offered the chance to hit the ball from the centre front of the court (*Diagram 9*), he or she is ideally placed for a crack to *n* in the hope that the ball will rebound into the nick and die. Note how B's position partially obscures A from the ball

This is where a little spin or slice can come in useful – by making the ball hug the side wall. However, such returns seldom win the point outright, even if they rarely concede the rally to the next shot hit by your opponent.

A close study of that 1977 Open Championship final between Hunt and Nancarrow showed a ratio of straight to cross-court shots of about three to one. Few points ended directly because of the straight shots but most rallies were brought to a conclusion when a less than perfect straight shot let one or other man hit a really effective, court-opening, cross-court placement. Alternatively, a series of successive down-the-wall shots was broken by a cross-court lob of a length necessary to prevent such world-class players making a really aggressive overhead shot.

Drop Shots

In squash, as in all games, the word 'never' is out of place. No matter how much it may be against every book there ever was, the time when the 'wrong' shot is right must arise occasionally. So in using the word 'never' I have kept in mind the once-in-a-thousand occasion when the dictum should be ignored.

Nevertheless, in the case of the drop shot, do not try it when your opponent is nearer to the front wall than you are except, perhaps, when he or she has already been forced forwards with one drop shot and is haring for the back wall in expectation of a following lob. In that and other wrong-footing situations your drop shot may win the point outright but the primary virtues of such

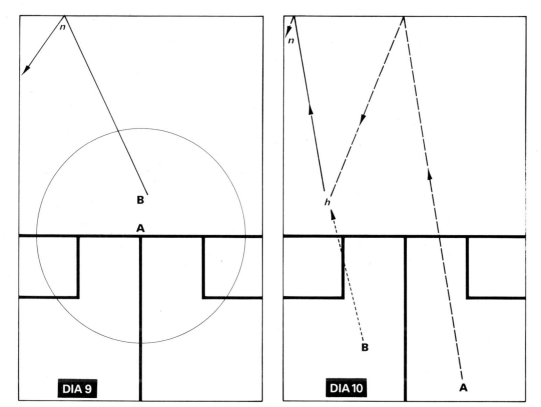

DIA 9

DIA 10

shots are the creation of openings and the tiring of your opponent. So far as the former is concerned, the drop shot is most effective when the ball is new and cold and its bounce limited. When constant thrashing against the walls has hotted it up, its bounce will become longer and livelier so giving your opponent extra time to reach it and make effective replies.

Ideally, then, use your drop shot when you are in front of the short line. This means your racket will often be around shoulder height. Try to strike the ball when it is between you and the side wall: firstly, to give yourself room to swing your racket sweetly and, secondly, so that you will not be knocked over or in the way when your opponent hurtles forward. Few things are more galling than making a superb drop shot only to have a let awarded against you because you were in your opponent's way.

The ball should travel downwards to hit the front wall just above the board so that it rebounds into the side-wall nick 457 millimetres (18 inches) or so away; see Diagram 10. Though the stroke you make is soft, it must still be firm and without any tentative drawing-back. The racket handle should be held firmly, the wrist braced, and power reduced by the severe restriction of your backswing; the stroke is more of a push than an actual swing. Theoretically, underspin will help the ball to 'die' after hitting the floor but be sparing in the amount you use. Racket-head control is so vital and the movement relatively so small that trying for spin makes great demands on timing. Better to keep your racket head

Diagram 10: The drop shot. B anticipates a straightforward return and bounds forward to *h*, hitting a soft yet purposeful shot aimed to make the ball hit the front wall just above the tin and then into the nick at *n*, about 450 millimetres (18 inches) from the front wall

The right and wrong way to make a drop shot return. The left-hand player shapes to hit powerfully while taking a giant step forward, only to stay low, checking the swing to drop the ball softly onto the front wall. There is no pulling back. The stroke may be soft but it is firm and positive

lined up with the intended path of the ball throughout your stroke.

Keep your weight forward so that your nose is well over the ball when you hit it. Apart from partially disguising your intentions, this mitigates against a natural tendency to pull back from the ball when trying any soft shot. Remembering what Euclid said about a straight line, direct most of your drop shots towards the front and nearest side wall, trying always to make the ball drop off that front wall into the nick.

Strive to 'feel' the ball with your fingers rather than the fleshy part of your hand where your fingers begin. Whether static or moving, maintain good balance and hit the ball so that your racket face 'chases' it along the same line; this helps to standardize your sensations of touch. Start your swing with your wrist cocked as for a natural drive but straighten rather than snap it at impact. This will help softness of touch. Having played your drop shot, move sideways and away before hurrying once more for your strategic position at the 'T'.

Though the aim when drop-shotting may be the nick, it is only achieved about 20% of the time. The other 80% of attempts result in the ball rebounding so that it can be kept in play. How well depends on how near it remains to the front and side wall, how low it bounces, and whether it has surprised or outmanoeuvred your opponent. But the drop shot has another advantage too. A thoughtful, positive mixture of drop shots and deep lobs can significantly sap an opponent's stamina, so reducing resistance towards the end of a long match.

Lobs

Sometimes it is tactically a good ploy to incorporate an upward wrist snap into your swing and hoist the ball in a lob over your opponent's head to the back wall when he or she is positive you are about to drop the ball short; see Diagram 11. Remember to

vary the height of your lobs. If your opponent is rushing forward, you may well score outright with a low lob that just clears his or her head without falling particularly deep. At other times your object may be more defensive, in which case aim deep . . . but not so deep that the ball hits the back wall before bouncing because that will merely send it back into mid-court in a position favourable to your opponent. The ideal lob has the ball bouncing to fall near the back wall. Such lobs are usually even more effective if the ball is also tucked into the side.

The length from the out-of-court line at the junction of the front and one side wall to the floor at the junction of the back and other side wall is 12·88 metres (42 feet 3 inches). That is an extra 3·05 metres (10 feet) compared with a drive straight from front to back wall. It therefore makes sense to use the diagonal lob in

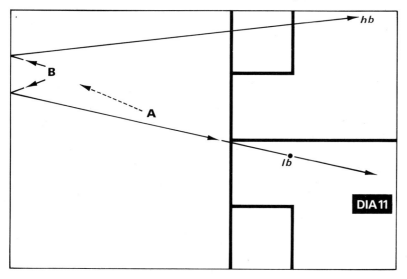

Diagram 11: A subtle use of the lob. A has played a drop shot and is following B forward in anticipation of a similar reply. If B is alert and quick, he or she may well win the point outright with a fast, low lob which just clears and wrong-foots A, bouncing at *lb*. If the drop shot is too good or B is a shade slow, his or her best answer will probably be a high lob which hugs the side wall and lands at *hb*

There is a lot of room up in the air and lobs are a valuable way of moving your opponent backwards, especially when he or she has just scrambled a ball from up front. The lob is a firm, strong shot, with the racket coming slightly under the ball and the head and shoulders staying down. The eyes should never lead or leave the ball

defensive situations and one straight down the wall when time and position permit you to think more aggressively.

Again, the lob demands a firm, positive mental attitude and stroke. As when making a drop shot, avoid pulling your body away from the ball at impact. Changes in length and height are achieved by modifying the swing of the stroke and by sensitive variations of touch in your hand and, above all, fingers. Avoid the natural tendency to jerk your head and shoulders upwards just before or at the moment of impact. Head and shoulders down, please, until the stroke is completed. Obtain altitude by a slight change in the plane of your swing and by using wrist snap in the zip area of that swing. However, the overriding importance of getting every ball back, no matter how impossible it may seem, will inevitably result in scooping rather than stroking the ball upwards now and then.

Angles and Reverse Angles

An angle is a shot which hits a side wall before going on to the front wall. Thus in Diagram 12 A's shot 1 to the nearside wall is an angle and shot 2 to the wall nearer to B is a 'reverse angle'. Both are attacking shots, used to introduce a surprise element into the rally. By choosing to hit one or other side wall with a fast, aggressive drive you can break up any anticipated pattern of return.

The 'ordinary' angle should hit the nearside wall somewhere in front of the short line. Try always to keep the ball down so that its bounce after hitting the front wall will be low and difficult to reach. Strive also to mask the direction of your stroke.

The reverse angle is probably the most spectacular shot in the game. It was the speciality of Mike Oddy, the British amateur champion in 1961 and 1962 and one of the few amateurs of the past twenty years to reach the English Open Championship final. He used the shot particularly well when returning service. Quick

Diagram 12: Angles. Shot 1 is an aggressive side-wall angle shot used to draw an opponent away from the 'T', whereas shot 2, the reverse angle, achieves the same effect with a greater element of surprise

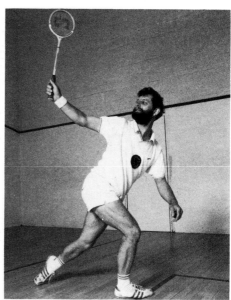

to spot loose serves, he used to bound forwards to hit the ball along the line *rr* in Diagram 13.

   This is a difficult, adventurous shot, carrying with it several real advantages: your opponent should be on or moving towards the 'T' as you make the stroke so the ball flashes across his or her line of

Diagram 13: The reverse angle. R (the receiver) 'reads' the serve quickly, hurries forward, and from *h* hits the ball along line *rr*, while the server (S) is moving to the 'T'

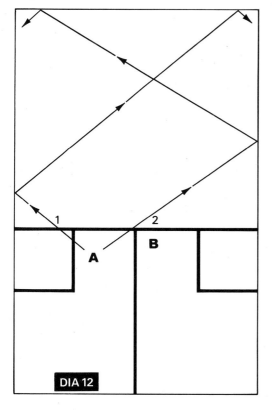

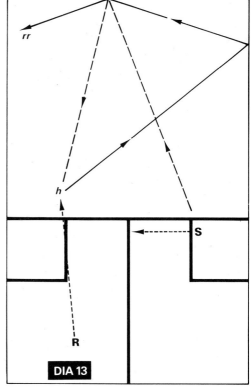

The surprise element in a reverse angle drive. The player in the back court is anticipating a down-the-wall drive but is wrong footed by the sudden pulling of the ball across his opponent's body. It hits the left wall, bounds onto the front, and then travels across court in the opposite direction to the back-court player's run. That player loses sight of the ball when it crosses the striker's body and again when he runs for the side wall

vision, instead of along it as with other returns, and it is also travelling in front of your opponent's last focal point, namely the front wall. Both factors contribute to the difficulty of perceiving the flight of the ball correctly. Instinctively your opponent may tend to move in the direction of its flight, hence wrong-footing, and the overall path of the ball takes it farther away from the receiver than any return other than the down-the-wall drop shot already described.

Another advantage is that your stroke preparation and forward swing tend to be concealed from your opponent by your body. Inherent in this is a particular danger: you are hitting more across the line of the oncoming ball than with any other stroke so your timing has to be ultra precise if you are to avoid erring or presenting your opponent with a 'sitter' because of poor direction. Yet timed precisely and hit at the correct angle and pace it is a prolific point-winner . . . and a most exciting shot to make. If you really enjoy shot-making, give this one plenty of practice. If you are strictly a 'play the percentages' disciple, treat it with the greatest possible caution.

The Boast

One addictive and mainly defensive shot used fairly prolifically in rally play is called the 'boast', and it comes in three varieties: single wall, double wall, and back wall. Whichever it is, nine times out of ten it is hit only because the player is under intense pressure and probably unable to see the front wall. By implication, therefore, a boast is played when you have been forced back and into a corner and the only way to keep the ball in play is to hit it hard onto the side wall so it rebounds forwards onto the front wall. This is the simple, 'single-wall boast'. Occasionally, your position may be so bad that you cannot even make the angle that will send the ball onto the front wall off one side wall. Such a situation calls for the 'double-wall boast', when you are forced to zigzag the ball off first one side wall and then the other to keep it going over the tin. Worst of all, you may have been lured up court and then hustled backwards by a lob that is not going to rebound sufficiently off the back wall for you to hit it forwards. Thus, you may have no alternative but to play the 'back-wall boast', slamming the ball against the back wall in order to bounce it up onto the front wall. All too frequently this will be the last shot you make in the rally since your return will be so weak that your opponent will have no difficulty in killing the ball.

Stroke technique varies little from that used for normal strokes. But since you are likely to be hurrying backwards and away from the direction in which you have hit the ball, there is little chance of adding forward body-momentum to your swing. You must compensate by exaggerating your shoulder-to-the-back-wall posture in order to pivot strongly towards the front when you swing at the ball.

However, you are still bound to lose some power and this is further decreased by the energy squandered in heat during the impact of the ball on the side wall. Obviously you need something to help the ball lift off it. Turn again to the section on spin (page 37) and examine the behaviour of a ball when topspin is imparted to it. Note how it rolls the ball upwards when it strikes a wall. Many, perhaps most, boasts are struck with topspin. But remember that topspin also lifts the ball off the floor and your opponent will relish that. So make sure you keep your head down until you have actually hit the ball. Then do not waste a single millisecond before hastening towards the 'T'.

Diagram 14 on page 50 illustrates a typical situation. Your opponent (A) has forced you (B) forward and right before sending you back towards the other side wall. You chase the ball and catch it up at h. Your back is three quarters turned towards the front wall and you are at full stretch; whether your left or right side is nearer to the ball depends on the distance and speed of your chase. Any thoughts about correct footwork are out of the question. Your primary aim is to keep the rally going: your solution a boast off the side wall and your only method of developing the necessary power a strong shoulder pivot.

If you are very quick and unthinking you may be able to reach far enough behind the ball to thump it towards point x, on the side wall. However, its subsequent path, $x1$, takes it at a near perfect angle for A to kill it into the forehand nick.

A better solution would be to play the ball strongly onto the side wall at y so that it rebounds onto the front wall and then, if you are lucky, into the nick. This is by no means an unsuccessful reply because, even if the ball does not die in the nick, it does at least succeed in drawing A away from the 'T', although he or she should not really have that much difficulty in reaching the ball.

But an even more effective solution would be to aim at z with a good-length shot which hugs the side wall and forces A to the

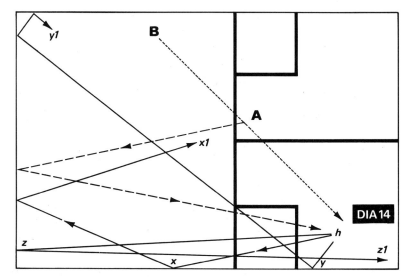

Diagram 14: The boast. Three of B's possible responses to A's front-wall drive. Note how differences in where the boast hits the side wall have big effects on the subsequent direction of the ball

back of the court, hopefully presenting him or her with a similar problem.

Whether you are playing a single- or double-wall boast, you will be in a hurry and hurry is not conducive to micrometrically accurate geometrical calculations. Nevertheless, the walls do not move so if you can maintain a clear mental picture of your position and have practised boasting quietly on your own, you may produce better angles than expected. Remember, however, that although the walls are a constant which you can rely upon, your opponent moves and is eager to end the rally. The temptation is to watch him or her rather than mentally computing those movements, out-thinking the player, and then concentrating fiercely on the ball. All this in no way denies the fact that you will be in an inferior court position and that your main aim must be to keep the ball in play as best you can.

Return of Service

Variety of height, direction, and placement are just as essential in returning service as in all other aspects of rally play. Power is valuable but can be self-destructive if used indiscriminately. Your primary objectives should be to wrest the initiative from the server while remaining intensely alert for a chance of pouncing on a loose serve and hitting an immediate winner. Secondary to these two aims should come your determination, when pressurized, to temporize with your return so that the server cannot improve upon an already attacking position. No matter how much the serve has tied you up, get the ball in play somehow: a deep, high lob is unlikely to worsen the position significantly and will probably give you at least one more chance to stay in play and keep the rally going.

The server will be striving to force or subtly winkle out a weak return in order to increase the strength of his or her following shot. The receiver's concentration and effort should be focussed intently on seizing the attack or, at least, on replying with a temporizing shot – a high lob down the side wall, perhaps – anything which does not reinforce the superior position inherent when serving.

Most serves from the right-hand court will be made from your opponent's forehand side so your view of the racket and ball at the moment of impact will be restricted. When service is made from the left-hand court you will probably have a much better view since forehand services will be hit when both body and swing are towards you. Learn to 'read' the clues revealed by body position, racket swing, throw, eyes, and so on. Then, fractionally before the ball is struck, switch 100% attention to the server's racket face and ball. Peak your concentration at that moment so that you can 'pick' the direction, height, and speed of the ball at the earliest possible moment. Only in that way can you seize every tiny chance of immediately wresting the attack from the server.

Reactions to sound are around 30% faster than they are to visual stimulation so listen perceptively and compute what you hear with what you see. All this must take place in something like 500 milliseconds but objective assessment of sound can save you around 100 of those milliseconds and in a fast game like squash that can actually be the difference between an ultimately winning and losing return.

Sustain that intensity of perception until you have made your reply. This should not imply any lack of concentration thereafter but that sort of intensity cannot be maintained for more than a couple of seconds so a skilled player will learn to summon those supreme heights at the critical moments of each rally. These normally occur during the zip-area section of an opponent's stroke. This may sound tremendously theoretical and to some degree it is. Yet great players do develop this slightly undulating pattern of concentration, possibly through application and certainly helped enormously by experience, though it is extremely doubtful if they are aware of what they are doing. However, the purpose of practice is to convert controlled, complex movements into automatic reflexes and this can apply to the learning of effective concentration too.

Just as the server should be seeking for clever variations so should the receiver vary the returns of service. Basically, you have the choice of five shots: down the side wall, across the court, the drop shot, the reverse angle, or the lob. All have been covered in this chapter and need little amplification other than a reminder that unlike the subsequent rally you will not have directly influenced the preceding shot. The server will have chosen the pace, height, and angle of delivery so the likelihood is that you will be in a slightly defensive position. You can counter this to some degree by mental alertness and speed of positioning. When in doubt, temporize with either a down-the-wall return or a lob, but do occasionally chance a reverse-angle return. Even at the

Diagram 15: Graphs showing the improved performance of a league soccer team in the later stages of play when Dynamo (a high-intensive glucose syrup) has maintained the blood-sugar content in the brain. These figures are based on a cumulative analysis of twenty games.

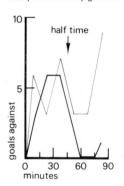

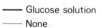
Glucose solution
None

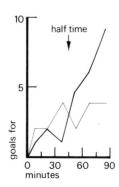

Domination of the 'T': a rally sequence demonstrating the tactical importance of holding that part of the court. Player B is most easily distinguished by the contrasting trim at collar and sleeve

Top row: Having served, A moves to the 'T' (left), keeping an eye on the actions of B, who plays a shot to the backhand front corner. A then retrieves the ball (right), while B gains the 'T'. In order to force B away from the 'T', A plays an across-court lob deep into the forehand back corner

Centre row: Whilst B is moving to play his shot from the forehand back corner (left), A, watching closely, returns to the 'T'. Note that A has had time to reach the 'T' before B actually plays his shot. B has attempted to play the ball down the forehand side wall to a good length but is not very accurate. A cuts the ball off (right) but, as he does not really have B out of position yet, he in turn plays a good-length shot down the forehand side wall

Bottom row: B, having again been driven to the forehand back corner (left), is now forced to play a side-wall boast, which is spotted by A, who is watching closely. A moves quickly and easily to play a winning drop shot (right), while B is left stranded at the back of the court

highest levels there is much to be gained psychologically from injecting a little adventure and fun into the game.

Doing the Unexpected

Alternating cross-court lobs and straight drop shots can tax your opponent's stamina severely but in critical moments, when the adrenalin is flowing freely, he or she will probably be stimulated to move and think swiftly and decisively. Undue emphasis on power in squash can, of course, prove ultimately self defeating: the ball keeps hopping round the court and your opponent can almost wait for it to come to him or her. Yet in a crisis, when both players are at their peaks of alertness, power, used suddenly and unexpectedly, can be a trusty weapon.

There is good reason why this is particularly true if an opponent is visibly tiring. It is widely known that lactic acid builds up in the muscles when strenuous exercise has brought on physical tiredness. But it is realised by only comparatively few that combined physical and mental tiredness reduces the blood-sugar content of the brain. This does not exercise any tremendously significant effect on primary concentration: in a squash sense, seeing the ball. But it does have some effect on such factors as judgment of length, something covered by secondary concentration. The major reduction in playing effectiveness arises from a drastic loss of tertiary concentration, that factor which governs awareness of what your opponent is doing while you are watching the ball and moving towards it to make your stroke.

A classic example can be found in soccer where so many decisive goals arise from surprise moves in the closing 3 or 4 minutes: see Diagram 15 on page 51. The attackers are stimulated by the 'fight or flight' flow of adrenalin and move swiftly, whereas the leading team lack this stimulation and consequently are less able to overcome tiredness. A defender, say, will still see the ball and move more or less correctly towards the spot where he intends to meet it. But that depletion of blood-sugar content will have seriously reduced his ability to sense or see the opposing striker slipping quickly round his blind side. So the ball does not reach him; the striker gathers it up in his stride before banging it past the goalkeeper for the equalizer or winning goal that makes tomorrow's headlines.

Similarly, in squash, a tired player suffers from a reduced blood-sugar content and is thus less capable of spotting and adapting to the unexpected. And few things are more unexpected than an opponent who slams the ball in, say, a reverse-angle drive after maybe ten shots have been played at a slower pace.

Reading the Game Quiz

All three photographs show a player's eye view of an opponent about to reply to a shot near the wall. In two of these situations, the player should be able to anticipate his opponent's reply and begin moving in the right direction. Which is the odd one out? What are the opponent's options in that situation?

Use the diagram on the left to indicate into which area of the court the player should move to take his opponent's reply. Answers and explanations on page 57.

```
 3          2          1



 6          5          4



 9          8          7
```

Chapter Six
Training for Fitness

Any discussion on the unexpected use of power against a tired opponent leads naturally to the general question of fitness. The tremendous successes of Britain's Jonah Barrington in the late 1960s and early 1970s are sufficient to prove the value of super fitness. So far as motor skills are concerned, he was in no way any better or more gifted than half a dozen kids you can find in almost any school playground. Neither was or is his ball-sense exceptional. He scored heavily by applying his extraordinary motivation to the acquisition of technical proficiency and outstanding physical fitness. Indeed, he was the first man I ever heard using the expression 'breaking the pain barrier'. His undeniably sound approach was to make practice and training ten times as difficult as any match he ever played. This entailed hitting hundreds and hundreds of identical shots until he could scarcely lift his racket and arm .. and then hitting a few more dozen. He would also run, jump, stretch, or whatever until the pain was shattering . . . and then force himself to intensify his efforts and fight his way past and through the pain . . . and again . . . and again.

But enough of Barrington. If you are similarly motivated, my words will merely reinforce your own beliefs and, perhaps, add to your determination to maintain them. It is likely, however, that your ambitions are more modest: to represent your county or club, perhaps; to win the club championship; to beat that slightly cocky chap in the next office; or simply to enjoy good health. All are perfectly laudable ambitions, even if they require slightly differing levels of physical and mental fitness.

There is one imperative which must be stressed. Take time to build up your level of general fitness. And always, but always, warm up adequately before starting to play. Spend 10 minutes or so in the changing room gently stretching leg, arm, and shoulder muscles; if possible, put in a little jogging with a few short sprints; gently massage your arms, calves, thighs, and shoulders; do a little twisting from side to side at the hips. That kind of preparation reduces the chances of tearing muscles through beginning too vigorously and also assists in that essential factor in confident form – a good start.

Whatever your standard of play, your normal stamina, speed, and suppleness are almost bound to be inadequate. This inadequacy may actually be at danger level if you are a middle-aged executive who has not exercised strenuously for fifteen to twenty years and who suddenly feels it necessary to regain some youthful fitness. The mere fact that you are an executive suggests that you are more competitive by nature than many of your peers so when you

Above and following page: Two sequences from Ken Woolcott's Popmobility routines. A senior coach with the British Amateur Athletic Board, Woolcott found that athletes worked harder if they did their training routines to pop music. Amateur sports players please note

get on court you could very easily extend yourself beyond your personal safety limits.

There is no short cut to general fitness and no better route than through jog-running. It is boring and time consuming but it gets the lungs working, pouring oxygen into your blood stream, and your heart pumping harder and faster in distributing that blood around your circulatory system. So begin your running programme this very night . . . but sensibly. Dress in suitable clothes, put on a wrist watch with a second hand and go to your front door. Run in any suitable direction away from your door for 1 minute; turn and run home again. Without making it too painful, do try to make yourself puff a little. Rub down quickly, preferably take a warm bath, followed by a warm drink – milk is fine – and then go to bed. Repeat the programme for about a week. Then increase the time to 1½ minutes out and later 2 minutes. Continue until you can run for, say, 10 minutes each way – 20 minutes in all. Then stabilize this at four times a week. Once you have reached 3 minutes each way, begin to mix your jogging pace with regular, 10-yard bursts of speed. To repeat, while not killing yourself with effort, do arrange your mixtures of sprints and slower running so that your heart pumps and your lungs gasp several times during each work-out.

If there are any doubts at all about your basic health, or if you are over 35 years old, be quite sure to have your doctor check your fitness before embarking on squash or any physical training programme. On no account take it for granted that you are OK. Exercise cannot hurt a sound heart but it will quickly winkle out any weaknesses, no matter how small.

Running should be supplemented by more specific exercises. What form they take and what degree of effort you put in will depend on your ambitions and your determination to achieve them. As the 1970s draw to an end the number of municipal recreational centres is greatly increasing. In Britain, for example, over 80% of the population are within reasonable reach of one or more suitable centres and most of them are staffed by people fully qualified to guide the averagely ambitious squash player in evolving a suitable training programme.

And what about smoking and drinking? Unequivocally, smoking is harmful. Even ignoring its irrefutable association with cancer, smoking undoubtedly impairs the efficiency of the lungs. Alcohol is another form of drug. A little may help relaxation but there is a danger that the one beer of today becomes two tomorrow, so leading on to excesses that increase body weight and reduce speed and clarity of thought. These, of course, are somewhat stern judgments which have more relevance to championship-level players than to the great majority of devotees. My aim is simply to lay out the options clearly. Moderation in all things is a main route to better living.

Of one thing I am quite certain, playing squash with a purpose

In the first sequence (shown on page 55) you swing your arms backwards alternately while bouncing on either foot. In the second (above), you take six high running steps forward and then six back, driving your arms and legs as if sprinting

is far more pleasurable than simply playing aimlessly. If you enjoy your games, you will play more frequently and if you play more frequently and thoughtfully you will improve more rapidly. That will bring more enjoyment . . . which is where we came in.

Answers to the Quiz

Situation 1

B is so near the back wall at x that he cannot get far enough behind the ball to return it down the wall and he is therefore forced to hit it onto the side wall so that A's next shot will probably be made in area 6.

Situation 2

A is at the 'T' but has hit a shot which makes it easy for B to get behind the ball at y. B's choice is almost limitless, with an angle to 6, a reverse angle which will probably go on into 4, a drop shot to 4, or a drive to 7 as probables.

Situation 3

A has played a good drop shot which has stretched B so far forward (to z) that he can only hit the ball at an angle onto the front wall where it will rebound towards 2, 3 or 6 if A does not cut off the ball with a volley.

Situations 1 and 3 demonstrate that extremes of length are advantageous. Situation 2 indicates that poor length leaves you wide open, even if you are on the 'T'. So it's Situation 2 which is the odd one out.

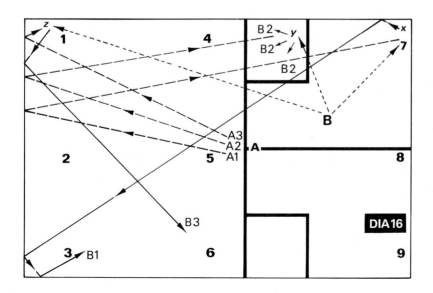

DIA 16

THE RULES OF THE SINGLES GAME

Approved by the International Squash Rackets Federation (ISRF) to be effective from 1st January, 1977. These rules refer to the game of Squash Rackets in respect of the game as played on courts, the specifications for which were first determined by The Squash Rackets Association (Great Britain). Reproduced by kind permission of The Squash Rackets Association.

1 THE GAME, HOW PLAYED. The game of Squash Rackets is played between two players with standard rackets, with balls officially approved by ISRF and in a rectangular court of standard dimensions, enclosed on all four sides.

2 THE SCORE. A match shall consist of the best of three or five games at the option of the promoters of the competition. Each game is 9 points up; that is to say, the player who first wins 9 points wins the game, except that, on the score being called 8-all for the first time, Hand-out may choose, before the next service is delivered, to continue the game to 10, in which case the player who first scores two more points wins the game. Hand-out must in either case clearly indicate his choice to the Marker, if any, and to his opponent.

Note to Referees. If Hand-out does not make clear his choice before the next service, the Referee shall stop play and require him to do so.

3 POINTS, HOW SCORED. Points can only be scored by Hand-in. When a player fails to serve or to make a good return in accordance with the rules, the opponent wins the stroke. When Hand-in wins a stroke, he scores a point; when Hand-out wins a stroke, he becomes Hand-in.

4 THE RIGHT TO SERVE. The right to serve first is decided by the spin of a racket. Thereafter the server continues to serve until he loses a stroke, when his opponent becomes the server, and so on throughout the match.

5 SERVICE. The ball before being struck shall be dropped or thrown in the air and shall not touch the walls or floor. The ball shall be served direct on to the front wall, so that on its return, unless volleyed, it would fall to the floor in the back quarter of the court opposite to the server's box from which the service has been delivered.

At the beginning of each game and of each hand, the server may serve from either box, but after scoring a point he shall then serve from the other, and so on alternately as long as he remains Hand-in or until the end of the game. If the server serves from the wrong box, there shall be no penalty and the service shall count as if served from the correct box, except that Hand-out may, if he does not attempt to take the service, demand that it be served from the other box.

A player with the use of only one arm may utilise his racket to project the ball into the air.

6 GOOD SERVICE. A service is good which is not a fault or which does not result in the server serving his

hand-out in accordance with Rule 9. If the server serves one fault, he shall serve again.

7 FAULT. A service is a fault (unless the server serves his hand-out under Rule 9):
  (a) If the server fails to stand with at least one foot on the floor within, and not touching the line surrounding the service box at the moment of striking the ball (called a foot fault).
  (b) If the ball is served on to, or below, the cut line.
  (c) If the ball served first touches the floor on, or in front of, the short line.
  (d) If the ball served first touches the floor outside the quarter of the court permitted for a good service in Rule 5.

8 FAULT, IF TAKEN. Hand-out may take a fault. If he attempts to do so, the service thereupon becomes good and the ball continues in play. If he does not attempt to do so, the ball shall cease to be in play, provided that, if the ball, before it bounces twice upon the floor, touches the server or anything he wears or carries, the server shall lose the stroke.

9 SERVING HAND-OUT. The server serves his hand-out and loses the stroke:
  (a) If the ball is served on to, or below, the board, or out, or against any part of the court before the front wall;
  (b) If the ball is not dropped or thrown in the air, or touches the wall or floor before being struck, or if he fails to strike the ball, or strikes it more than once;
  (c) If he serves two consecutive faults;
  (d) If the ball, before it has bounced twice upon the floor, or has been struck by his opponent touches the server or anything he wears or carries.

10 LET. A let is an undecided stroke, and the service or rally, in respect of which a let is allowed, shall not count and the server shall serve again from the same box. A let shall not annul a previous fault.

11 THE PLAY. After a good service has been delivered, the players return the ball alternately until one or other fails to make a good return, or the ball otherwise ceases to be in play in accordance with the rules.

12 GOOD RETURN. A return is good if the ball, before it has bounced twice upon the floor is returned by the striker on to the front wall above the board, without touching the floor or any part of the striker's body or clothing, provided the ball is not hit twice or out.

NOTE TO REFEREES

It shall not be considered a good return if the ball touches the board before or after it hits the front wall.

13 STROKES, HOW WON. A player wins a stroke:
  (a) Under Rule 9;
  (b) If the opponent fails to make a good return of the ball in play;

(c) If the ball in play touches his opponent or anything he wears or carries, except as is otherwise provided by Rules 14 and 15.

(d) If a stroke is awarded by the Referee as provided for in the Rules.

14 HITTING AN OPPONENT WITH THE BALL.
If an otherwise good return of the ball has been made, but before reaching the front wall it hits the striker's opponent, or his racket, or anything he wears or carries, then:

(a) If the ball would have made a good return, and would have struck the front wall without first touching any other wall, the striker shall win the stroke, except if the striker shall have followed the ball round, and so turned, before playing the ball, a let shall be allowed.

(b) If the ball would otherwise have made a good return, a let shall be allowed;

(c) If the ball would not have made a good return, the striker shall lose the stroke.

The ball shall cease to be in play, even if it subsequently goes up.

15 FURTHER ATTEMPTS TO HIT THE BALL.
If the striker strikes at, and misses the ball, he may make further attempts to return it. If, after being missed, the ball touches his opponent, or his racket, or anything he wears or carries, then:

(a) If the striker would otherwise have made a good return, a let shall be allowed;

(b) If the striker could not have made a good return, he loses the stroke.

If any such further attempt is successful, but the ball, before reaching the front wall, hits the striker's opponent, or his racket, or anything he wears or carries, a let shall be allowed, and Rule 14a shall not apply.

16 APPEALS

(a) An appeal may be made against any decision of the Marker, except for (b) (i) and (ii) below.

(b) (i) No appeal shall be made in respect of foot faults.

(ii) No appeal shall be made in respect of the Marker's call of 'fault' to the first service.

(iii) If the Marker calls 'fault' to the second service, the server may appeal, and if the decision is reversed, a let shall be allowed.

(iv) If the Marker allows the second service, Hand-out may appeal, either immediately, or at the end of the rally, if he has played the ball, and if the decision is reversed, Hand-in becomes Hand-out.

(v) If the Marker does not call 'fault' to the first service, Hand-out may appeal that the service was a fault, provided he makes no attempt to play the ball. If the Marker does not call 'Out' or 'Not up' to the first service, Hand-out may appeal, either immediately or at the end of the rally, if he has played the ball. In either case, if the appeal is disallowed, Hand-out shall lose the stroke.

(c) An appeal under Rule 12 shall be made at the end of the rally.

(d) In all cases where an appeal for a let is desired, this appeal shall be made by addressing the Referee with the words 'Let, please'. Play shall thereupon cease until the Referee has given his decision.

(e) No appeal may be made after the delivery of a service for anything that occurred before that service was delivered.

17 FAIR VIEW AND FREEDOM TO PLAY THE BALL.

(a) After playing a ball, a player must make every effort to get out of his opponent's way. That is:

(i) A player must make every effort to give his opponent a fair view of the ball, so that he may sight it adequately for the purpose of playing it.

(ii) A player must make every effort not to interfere with, or crowd, his opponent in the latter's attempt to get to, or play, the ball.

(iii) A player must make every effort to allow his opponent, as far as the latter's position permits, freedom to play the ball directly to the front wall, or side walls near the front wall.

(b) If any such form of interference has occurred and, in the opinion of the Referee, the player has not made every effort to avoid causing it, the Referee shall on appeal, or without waiting for an appeal, award the stroke to his opponent.

(c) However, if interference has occurred, but in the opinion of the Referee, the player has made every effort to avoid causing it, the Referee shall on appeal, or may without waiting for an appeal, award a let, except that if his opponent is prevented from making a winning return by such interference or by distraction from the player, the Referee shall award the stroke to the opponent.

(d) When in the opinion of the Referee, a player refrains from playing the ball, which, if played, would clearly and undoubtedly have won the rally under the terms of Rule 14(a), he shall be awarded the stroke.

NOTE TO REFEREES

(i) The practice of impeding an opponent in his efforts to play the ball by crowding or obscuring his view, is highly detrimental to the game, and Referees should have no hesitation in enforcing paragraph (b) above.

(ii) The words 'interfere with' in (a)(ii) above must be interpreted to include the case of a player having to wait for an excessive swing of his opponent's racket.

18 LET, WHEN ALLOWED.
Notwithstanding anything contained in these rules, and provided always that the striker could have made a good return:

(a) A let may be allowed:

(i) If, owing to the position of the striker, his opponent is unable to avoid being touched by the ball before the return is made.

NOTES TO REFEREES

This rule shall be construed to include the cases of the striker, whose position in front of his opponent makes it

59

impossible for the latter to see the ball, or who shapes as if to play the ball and changes his mind at the last moment, preferring to take the ball off the back wall, the ball in either case hitting his opponent, who is between the striker and the back wall. This is not, however, to be taken as conflicting in any way with the Referee's duties under Rule 17.

    (ii) If the ball in play touches any articles lying in the court.

    (iii) If the striker refrains from hitting the ball owing to a reasonable fear of injuring his opponent.

    (iv) If the striker, in the act of playing the ball, touches his opponent.

    (v) If the Referee is asked to decide an appeal and is unable to do so.

    (vi) If the player drops his racket, calls out or in any other way distracts his opponent, and the Referee considers that such occurrence has caused the opponent to lose the stroke.

(b) A Let shall be allowed:

    (i) If Hand-out is not ready, and does not attempt to take the service.

    (ii) If a ball breaks during play.

    (iii) If an otherwise good return has been made, but the ball goes out of court on its first bounce.

    (iv) As provided for in Rules 14, 15, 16(b)(iii), 23 and 24.

(c) No let shall be allowed if the player makes an attempt to play the ball except as provided for under Rules 15, 18(a)(iv), 18(b)(ii) and 18(b)(iii).

(d) Unless an appeal is made by one of the players, no let shall be allowed except where these rules definitely provide for a let, namely, Rules 14(a) and (b), 17 and 18(b)(ii) and (iii).

19 NEW BALL. At any time, when the ball is not in actual play, a new ball may be substituted by mutual consent of the players, or, on appeal by either player, at the discretion of the Referee.

20 KNOCK-UP

(a) The Referee shall allow on the court of play to either player, or to the two players together, a period not exceeding five minutes, or two and a half minutes each, immediately preceding the start of play for the purpose of knocking-up. In the event of a separate knock-up, the choice of knocking-up first shall be decided by the spin of a racket. The Referee shall allow a further period for the players to warm the ball up if the match is being resumed after a considerable delay.

(b) Where a new ball has been substituted under Rule 18(b)(ii) or 19, the Referee shall allow the ball to be knocked-up to playing condition. Play shall resume on the direction of the Referee, or prior mutual consent of the players.

(c) Between games the ball shall remain on the floor of the court in view and knocking-up shall not be permitted except by consent of the players.

21 PLAY IN A MATCH IS TO BE CONTINU-OUS. After the first service is delivered, play shall be continuous so far as is practical, provided that:

(a) At any time play may be suspended owing to bad light or other circumstances beyond the control of the players, for such period as the Referee shall decide. In the event of play being suspended for the day, the match shall start afresh, unless both players agree to the contrary.

(b) The Referee shall award a game to the opponent of any player, who, in his opinion persists, after due warning, in delaying the play in order to recover his strength and wind, or for any other reason.

(c) An interval of one minute shall be permitted between games and of two minutes between the fourth and fifth games of a five-game match. A player may leave the court during such intervals, but shall be ready to resume play at the end of the stated time. When ten seconds of the interval permitted between games are left, the Marker shall call 'Ten seconds' to warn the players to be ready to resume play. Should either player fail to do so when required by the Referee, a game may be awarded to his opponent.

(d) In the event of an injury, the Referee may require a player to continue play or concede the match, except where the injury is contributed to by his opponent, or where it was caused by dangerous play on the part of the opponent. In the former case, the Referee may allow time for the injured player to receive attention and recover, and in the latter, the injured player shall be awarded the match under Rule 24(c)(ii).

(e) In the event of a ball breaking, a new ball may be knocked-up, as provided for in Rule 20(b).

NOTES TO REFEREES

    (i) In allowing time for a player to receive attention and recover, the Referee should ensure that there is no conflict with the obligation of a player to comply with Rule 21(b), that is, that the effects of the injury are not exaggerated and used as an excuse to recover strength and wind.

    (ii) The Referee should not interpret the words 'contributed to' by the opponent to include the situation where the injury to the player is a result of that player occupying too close a position to his opponent.

22 CONTROL OF A MATCH. A match is normally controlled by a Referee, assisted by a Marker. One person may be appointed to carry out the functions of both Referee and Marker. When a decision has been made by a Referee, he shall announce it to the players and the Marker shall repeat it with the subsequent score.

Up to one hour before the commencement of a match either player may request a Referee and Marker other than appointed, and this request may be considered and a substitute appointed. Players are not permitted to request any such change after the commencement of a match, unless both agree to do so. In either case the decision as to whether an official is to be replaced or not must remain in the hands of the Tournament Referee, where applicable.

23 DUTIES OF MARKER.

(a) The Marker calls the play and the score, with the server's score first. He shall call 'Fault', 'Foot-Fault', 'Out' or 'Not up' as appropriate.

(b) If in the course of play the Marker calls 'Not up' or 'Out' or in the case of a second service 'Fault' or 'Foot Fault' then the rally shall cease.

(c) If the Marker's decision is reversed on appeal, a let shall be allowed, except as provided for in Rule 24(b)(iv) and (v).

(d) Any service or return shall be considered good unless otherwise called.

(e) After the server has served a fault, which has not been taken, the Marker shall repeat the score and add the words 'One fault', before the server serves again. This call should be repeated should subsequent rallies end in a let, until the point is finally decided.

(f) When no Referee is appointed, the Marker shall exercise all the powers of the Referee.

(g) If the Marker is unsighted or uncertain, he shall call on the Referee to make the relevant decision; if the latter is unable to do so, a let shall be allowed.

24 DUTIES OF REFEREE.

(a) The Referee shall award Lets and Strokes and make decisions where called for by the rules, and shall decide all appeals, including those against the Marker's calls and decisions. The decision of the Referee shall be final.

(b) He shall in no way intervene in the Marker's calling except:
  (i) Upon appeal by one of the players.
  (ii) As provided for in Rule 17.
  (iii) When it is evident that the score has been incorrectly called, in which case he should draw the Marker's attention to the fact.
  (iv) When the Marker has failed to call the ball 'Not up' or 'Out' and on appeal he rules that such was in fact the case, the stroke should be awarded accordingly.
  (v) When the Marker has called 'Not up' or 'Out' and on appeal he rules that this was not the case, a Let shall be allowed except that if in the Referee's opinion, the Marker's call had interrupted an undoubted winning return, he shall award the stroke accordingly.
  (vi) The Referee is responsible that all times laid down in the rules are strictly adhered to.

(c) In exceptional cases, the Referee may order:
  (i) A player, who has left the court, to play on.
  (ii) A player to leave the court and to award the match to the opponent.
  (iii) A match to be awarded to a player whose opponent fails to be present in court within ten minutes of the advertised time of play.
  (iv) Play to be stopped in order to warn that the conduct of one or both of the players is leading to an infringement of the rules. A Referee should avail himself of this rule as early as possible when either player is showing a tendency to break the provisions of Rule 17.

(d) If after a warning a player continues to contravene Rule 20(c) the Referee shall award a game to the opponent.

25 COLOUR OF PLAYERS' CLOTHING.

For amateur events under the control of the ISRF, players are required to wear all white clothing, provided however, the ISRF officers at their sole discretion can waive compliance with this rule.

Member countries of the ISRF may legislate, if they so desire, to allow clothing of a light pastel colour to be worn for all other events under their control

The Referee's decision thereon is final.

Note: Footwear is deemed clothing for this rule.

NOTES TO PLAYERS AND OFFICIALS

Incorporating ISRF Rule Changes, in which basically the aim has been to tidy up the previous rules, make life easier for Referees by giving penalties they can award rather than extreme measures they are reluctant to impose, clarify the wording of some rules and in general work towards a code which can be interpreted consistently by officials in all member nations of the ISRF.

In order to assist players in understanding the correct application of the rules regarding marking and refereeing the following points are set out:–

1 **Under Rule 22:** DUTIES OF A MARKER. It is clearly stated that the control of the game is vested in the marker and it is his duty to call the play and the score.

2 **Under Rule 23:** THE REFEREE. A referee may be appointed **to whom all appeals shall be directed** including appeals against the marker's decisions and calls.

A referee may not normally interfere with the marker's counting of the game except upon appeal by one of the players, unless he is completely certain that the Marker has made an error in the calling of the score.

The exception to this is the provision of **Rule 17:** FAIR VIEW, where the referee may interpose a let or award a stroke if he considers that circumstances warrant such. In general no let shall be allowed unless an appeal is made by one of the players (see Rule 18).

In connection with the above it is stressed that markers and referees have been encouraged to enforce the provisions of Rule 17 bearing in mind that it is **"unnecessary obstruction"** which is penalised **irrespective of whether it is intentional or not.**

3 It is pointed out that where a marker only is in attendance he exercises all the powers of a referee and it is therefore considered to be in order for a player to direct an appeal to him **as referee** from any decision or calls made by him in his capacity **as marker.**

4 Anything in the nature of aggressive or temperamental appealing will not be tolerated by the SRA.

5 By noting these points it is hoped, NOT that players will habitually resort to indiscriminate appealing, but that they will achieve a better understanding of how to play to a referee.

Glossary

Ace A service which the receiver is unable to return.

Angle An aggressive shot onto the side wall facing the striker which rebounds onto the front wall.

Appeal A request against the marker's decision. The referee deals with all appeals.

Backhand A stroke made on the left-hand side of a right-handed player and so named because the back of the hand faces the ball at impact.

Backhand Court The left side of the court.

Back-Wall Boast A boast off the back wall onto the front wall.

Ball A squash ball is made from a composition of rubber and butyl and is hollow. The speed of the ball increases when warmed by play, but there are four different speeds, recognisable by a code of coloured dots. The object of the difference in speed is to keep the game at a constant pace regardless of the temperature in the court.

Boast A defensive shot played from an awkward position onto a side wall which then rebounds onto the front wall.

Check The speed of the racket can be 'checked' before impact to slow the pace of the ball in order to confuse the opponent with speed variation.

Clinger A shot played off the front wall which travels back along the side, 'clinging' to it. A clinger is difficult to return.

Crowding A player cramps an opponent's freedom of movement by standing too close or moving in after playing a shot.

Cut An underspin or slice applied to the ball so that it drops sharply on hitting the front wall.

Cut Line The line marked on the front wall at a height of 1·83 metres (6 feet), above which the service stroke must be played.

Cut Service A service stroke sliced severely to bring the ball down steeply near the back wall or into the nick.

Dead Nick A ball which bounces in the junction of the floor and a wall so that it does not rise. A dead nick is an outright winner.

Die A ball which loses momentum rapidly on impact is said to 'die' because it is often unplayable.

Double Boast A boast which hits both side walls or the back wall and one side wall before hitting the front wall.

Down Out of play. A ball which hits the tin or the play line is 'down'.

Drop Shot A shot which dies on impact with the front wall or close to it.

Drop Volley A drop shot played off a volley instead of after the bounce.

Fair View After making a stroke, a player must get out of the opponent's way as much as possible to allow a 'fair view' of the ball and freedom of stroke.

Fault A service which falls under the cut line, touches the floor on or in front of the short line, or strikes the wrong quarter of the court is called a fault. The receiver may choose to play a fault.

Floor Squash courts usually have sprung floors to eliminate jarring of the feet. Canadian maple is generally used because it is a hard, light-coloured wood.

Follow-Through The completion of the racket swing after impact.

Foot Fault A foot fault is called if the server fails to stand with at least one foot within and not touching the service-box line.

Forehand A stroke made on the right-hand side of a right-handed player. The front of the hand faces the ball at impact.

Gallery The viewing area for spectators, usually situated above the back wall. Some championship courts also have galleries above the side walls. Spectator seating was limited in the past but glass walls now make it possible to accommodate more spectators.

Game The first player to win nine points wins the game except when at 8-all the player receiving decides that the first player to score two more points should win.

Game Ball When the server needs one point to win the game, the marker calls 'game ball'.

Half-Court Line The line which runs parallel with the side walls from the back wall to the short line.

Half-Nick A shot that bounces unpredictably after hitting the junction between the floor and walls.

Half-Volley A stroke in which the ball hits the floor and racket virtually simultaneously.

Hand The period of play from the moment when a player becomes the server until he or she becomes the receiver.

Hand-In The player who is serving.

Hand-Out The player who is receiving. The marker also calls 'hand-out' when the server loses a rally and must give the serve to the receiver.

Interval The rest period between games during a match. The longest interval, usually of 1 or 2 minutes' duration falls between the fourth and fifth games.

Kill A stroke, usually containing slice, that makes it impossible to return the ball. A kill is frequently driven into the nick.

Knock-Up The 5-minute practice/warm-up period allowed to the players before a match.

Length A term used to describe where the ball bounces. A good-length ball bounces in the back 0·46 metres (18 inches) of the court; a poor-length ball is one which bounces near the short line.

Let The re-play of a rally because of a doubtful return, a denial of fair view, a player being hit by the ball or the racket, or obstruction.

Lob A stroke that lofts the ball over the opponent's head so that it drops into the back of the court.

Lob Service A service hit high onto the front wall so that the ball bounces just short of the back wall if not volleyed.

Marker An official appointed to control a match and call the score. The marker also exercises the referee's powers if no referee is appointed.

Masking The disguise of a stroke by the turn of the wrist just before impact to wrong foot the opponent.

Match Consists of the best of three or five games. Championship matches are always decided by the best of five games.

Match Ball The state of the match when the server requires one point to win is said to be 'match ball'.

Nick The junction of the floor and walls. 'Nick' also describes the shot that goes into this junction.

No Set The receiver can elect at 8-all that the winner of the next point shall win the game. This is often called 'sudden death'.

Not Up When the ball is struck after its second bounce or when it is not returned above the board in accordance with the rules, the marker calls 'not up' and the striker loses the rally.

Opening Up the Court Moving the ball and the opponent into an area of the court which leaves a large space into which to play a winner.

Out of Court A ball which touches any part outside the playing area, or any beams and girders or lights in the court roof, is 'out of court'. The lines marking the upper limits of the court are also defined as out of court.

Penalty Point In championship squash a penalty point is awarded when a player fails to give fair view of the ball and freedom of stroke to the opponent. The offending player loses the hand or, if he or she is receiving already, the point.

Play If a service is good, the marker calls 'play'. 'Play' is also called when the receiver plays a fault or when the marker wishes a rally to continue in spite of doubt by the players over a stroke.

Play Line The line marking the top of the tin which is sometimes angled and protrudes from the wall.

Point A point is won by the player who is hand-in and who wins a stroke.

Pull A disguised shot on which a player shapes for a straight shot but hits the ball slightly more in front of him or herself and so pulls it across the court.

Put Out A player who is hand-in is 'put out' when he or she loses the rally and must give the service to the opponent.

Quarter Court One part of the back half of the court which has been divided into two equal parts by the half-court line.

Racket The length of a squash racket must not exceed 685 millimetres (27 inches). The stringing area must not exceed 215 millimetres (8½ inches) in length and 184 millimetres (7¼ inches) in breadth. It must have a wooden framework in the head but the shaft may be made of steel, glass fibre, cane, laminated wood, etc.

Rally The continuous exchange of shots after the service until the ball is put out of play or a winner is struck.

Receiver The player who must return the service.

Referee An additional official usually appointed for championship events to assist the marker and to adjudicate. The referee awards lets or penalty points and may be appealed to by either player to reconsider decisions made by the marker. The referee deals with all appeals.

Reverse Angle An aggressive shot played across the court onto the wall to which the striker's back is turned.

Set When the score is 8-all, the marker reminds hand-out that before the next service he or she must decide whether to play the best of three points ('set two') or ask for 'no set' (the next point winning the game). If hand-out decides to play 'set two', he or she should indicate as much by putting up two fingers. The game cannot go beyond 10–9.

Short Line The line which runs parallel with the front and back walls at a distance of 5·49 metres (18 feet) from the front wall.

Side-Wall Boast *see* Boast

Side-Wall Smash A smash in which the ball is aimed to hit the side wall before the front wall.

Slice The application of a mixture of top- and sidespin, causing the ball to spin somewhere between its horizontal and vertical axes.

Smash A powerful, overhead stroke normally made at full stretch as an aggressive attack on a lobbed ball.

Stop Expression used by the referee to stop play.

Striker The player whose turn it is to hit the ball.

Stroke A stroke is won by the player whose opponent fails to serve or make a good return in accordance with the rules.

Sudden Death At 8-all hand-out may ask for 'no set', which is often called 'sudden death' because the next point wins the game.

The 'T' The centre of the court marked by the junction of the short and half-court lines. This is the area of the court from which it is easiest to control play.

Time Called by the marker to indicate that the 5-minute warm-up is over, to stop play, or to resume after the interval between games is over.

Tin The metal strip situated under the play line. This is usually composed of zinc and makes a resounding noise on impact to indicate that the shot is down.

Turning The action of a player who, unable to return the ball conventionally, must turn to follow the ball from the backhand to the forehand court (or vice versa) to play a stroke.

Two-Wall Boast *see* Double Boast

Up Any ball which does not hit the play line or the tin is said to be 'up' or in play.

Volley A stroke played before the ball has bounced.